THE
Spirit-Led
HEART

*Living
a Life of Love
and
Faith without
Borders*

SUZANNE ELLER

Foreword by Jennifer Dukes Lee

"I'm grateful for this deep—but somehow accessible—word. As a longtime Christ-follower, I have always had the desire, but not always the tools, to be led by the Spirit. I love this inspirational yet ever practical instruction in how to stop letting our hearts be tossed and turned by the whims of the world and instead be led by God himself. Not only has Suzie given us practical steps, but she's dared us to challenge our own limited thinking about who God is and how much he loves us."

Kathi Lipp, bestselling author, *The Husband Project*, *Overwhelmed*, and *Clutter Free*

"Join Suzie as she engages you with the Holy Spirit in a fresh way. She'll capture your heart, ignite your faith, and take it from routine to remarkable. Her invaluable teachings will challenge your convictions, redefine your choices, and sculpt you into the Spirit-filled woman God created you to be!"

Wendy Blight, author, *I Am Loved: Walking in the Fullness of God's Love*; writing team, First 5

"Sometimes, when we talk about what it means to have the Holy Spirit leading us in the steps of our lives, it can feel super mysterious . . . or weird . . . or emotional . . . or worrisome that we'll have to act out in some way we're unaccustomed to. Suzie Eller, through her devoted heart, with her encouraging and gentle voice, and as an experienced guide, breaks through those suppositions and will take you on an inspiring, equipping journey in *The Spirit-Led Heart*. With a beautiful blend of Bible history, personal stories, moments to stop and ponder, and encouragement to stand up and act, Suzie's newest book has taught me how to listen with greater intention, to learn with deeper understanding, and to seek the presence of the Holy Spirit with fresh eyes. This is a must-have guidebook for all of us who want to live our lives in closer alignment with the Spirit of God."

Julie Lyles Carr, author, *Raising an Original: Parenting Each Child according to Their Unique God-Given Temperament*; host, *The Modern Motherhood Podcast with Julie Lyles Carr*

"Voices from the extremes have left God's children unsure and missing out on the power of the Holy Spirit. Suzie defuses controversy with strong biblical teaching and her gentle voice. She pushes beyond denominational walls so that the lavish gift of God's Spirit can flood into every heart."

Amy Carroll, author, *Breaking Up with Perfect*;
speaker and writer, Proverbs 31 Ministries

"Inspiring and transforming! Consider *The Spirit-Led Heart* a beautiful journey of discovery. Suzie Eller invites us to spend time with the Holy Spirit so that we can know Him better. Receive her invitation and be awakened to the abundant wisdom, guidance, confidence, strength, and intimate relationship He offers. This book has a beautiful anointing that is undeniable."

Leah DiPascal, speaker and writer, Proverbs 31 Ministries;
writing team, First 5

"This book counseled and guided me as I was looking for direction. Suzie's ability to teach God's Word intersects with her transparent, vulnerable, and powerful life experiences. You'll wish you could dip the entire book into a bowl of highlighter ink! Thanks for helping me get back on track, Suzie!"

Christy Rodriguez, speaker and writer;
director and CEO, BraveGirlCommunity.com

"Suzie Eller invites the reader to sit down and engage in a grace-filled kitchen-table conversation that will change you and the way you see the world. Her thorough examination of Scripture encouraged and emboldened me to fully embrace the power of the Holy Spirit."

Lauren Snodgrass, community outreach coordinator,
Canopy Northwest Arkansas

"This book has changed the way I pray! The message Suzie writes has reminded me to invite the Holy Spirit to help in every area of my life, rather than try to live it in my own power. She speaks to just about every fear I've experienced and gently reminds me that, while in my own strength I fail, the Advocate is our Helper in every part of life. Suzie definitely writes from the 'me too' perspective and invites you into a journey along with her, with so much rich and specific direction to live a spirit-led life."

Casey Graves, church planter and lead pastor's wife,
Foundations Church, Tulsa, Oklahoma; author, *Perfectly Weak*

THE
Spirit - Led
HEART

Books by Suzanne Eller

Come with Me: Discovering the Beauty
of Following Where He Leads

Come with Me Devotional:
A Yearlong Adventure in Following Jesus

The Mended Heart: God's Healing for Your Broken Places

The Unburdened Heart: Finding the Freedom of Unforgiveness

The Spirit-Led Heart:
Living a Life of Love and Faith without Borders

THE

Spirit-Led

HEART

*Living a Life of Love
and Faith without Borders*

SUZANNE ELLER

BETHANYHOUSE
a division of Baker Publishing Group
Minneapolis, Minnesota

Published by Bethany House Publishers
11400 Hampshire Avenue South
Bloomington, Minnesota 55438
www.bethanyhouse.com

Bethany House Publishers is a division of
Baker Publishing Group, Grand Rapids, Michigan

Printed in the United States of America

ISBN 978-0-7642-3016-5

Library of Congress Control Number: 2017963592

Throughout, any emphasis in quoted Scripture has been added by the author.

Unless otherwise indicated, Scripture quotations are from the Holy Bible, New International Version®. NIV®. Copyright © 1973, 1978, 1984, 2011 by Biblica, Inc.™ Used by permission of Zondervan. All rights reserved worldwide. www.zondervan.com

Scripture quotations identified AMP are from the Amplified® Bible, copyright © 2015 by The Lockman Foundation. Used by permission. (www.Lockman.org)

Scripture quotations identified ESV are from The Holy Bible, English Standard Version® (ESV®), copyright © 2001 by Crossway, a publishing ministry of Good News Publishers. Used by permission. All rights reserved. ESV Text Edition: 2011

Scripture quotations identified MESSAGE are from THE MESSAGE. Copyright © by Eugene H. Peterson 1993, 1994, 1995, 1996, 2000, 2001, 2002. Used by permission of NavPress. All rights reserved. Represented by Tyndale House Publishers, Inc.

Scripture quotations identified NKJV are from the New King James Version®. Copyright © 1982 by Thomas Nelson, Inc. Used by permission. All rights reserved.

Scripture quotations identified NLT are from the Holy Bible, New Living Translation, copyright © 1996, 2004, 2015 by Tyndale House Foundation. Used by permission of Tyndale House Publishers, Inc., Carol Stream, Illinois 60188. All rights reserved.

Cover design by Emily Weigel

Author represented by The FEDD Agency, Inc.

18 19 20 21 22 23 24   7 6 5 4 3 2 1

CONTENTS

Contents

FOREWORD

Jennifer Dukes Lee

I have been feeling terribly weak. I habitually want to be strong and self-sufficient, but lately, I can't quite wrap my arms around everything that I am called to do in my marriage, my mothering, my job as a writer. I have long viewed myself as a high-capacity person, able to handle a lot in a day. But it isn't working anymore.

When things aren't working anymore, I don't generally give up. I generally put up a fight. I default to more self-sufficiency, more productivity. I work harder. I try to figure it all out on my own, thinking my own strength will satisfy all the demands on my life.

Surely, you sense the spiral here.

My bootstrap-pulling life has been getting me nowhere fast. A while back, I started to see the dark rings under my eyes, the way I was zoning out during dinner with my family. Turns out, my self-reliant nature was burning me out. I could sense it deep under my skin.

One morning, in my weakness, I dropped to my knees. That, it turns out, is the strongest place to be—kneeling before the Lord.

That morning, I cried out to the Holy Spirit to be fire and wind and power in my life. I confessed to him how I often ignore the person of the Holy Spirit. I confessed how often I have gone my own way, trusting my own power more than his. (Yes, I realize how ridiculous that sounds, once it's all typed out like that.) But that's the way I have so often lived—as a self-reliant woman instead of a God-reliant daughter.

When I prayed to the Holy Spirit that day, I felt his gentle conviction. But I also felt his enduring love for me. I was so moved by the goodness of God that I posted the entire prayer to Facebook that morning. I was pretty sure I wasn't the only one who needed to pray those words.

Thousands of people read that prayer over the next couple of days, including my friend Suzanne (Suzie) Eller. At the time, she was nearly finished writing the book you are now holding in your hands. That morning, she reached out to tell me she prayed that prayer with me. Because of the Holy Spirit, we were suddenly bonded by words in a prayer, and we both knew that our heart cry was the heart cry of women all over the world.

Suzie is like me. She is like you. She wants more of God's power in her life. But she also knows there are millions of women around the world who are missing out on this incredible gift that has been given to us: the Holy Spirit. That's why she wrote this beautiful book—a heartfelt primer on exploring the wild and wonderful spirit of God.

Like us, you want a Spirit-led heart instead of a self-led heart. You want more of that supernatural power, to give you the kind of strength and direction you could never muster on your own.

That's why Suzie and I are stretching our hands out to you. We invite you to pray that same prayer with us, and then, take the next step: Join Suzie on a terrific journey to encounter the Holy Spirit in a powerful new way.

The Prayer

Dear Holy Spirit,

I don't always pray to you. Maybe it's because you're harder to wrap my mind around. I "get" a Father. I relate to the person of Jesus. But Holy Spirit, you are wind and wandering and wild. You are breath. You come and go as you please, and sometimes you light upon my skin like a flame. You are presence, and you are power. I look back on my life and see startling evidence of your fingerprints; those are always the weak-kneed moments that make me go "Whoa."

You were present at creation, hovering over the waters, and you haven't left us since. You come to us through water and word, bread and wine. I find you at the altar—and on the floor. I find you in my deepest joys, and lingering around the edges of my heart when the pain is too much.

You kind of scare me, because you remind me that my self-sufficiency is worth nothing when you're around. You like me weak, and I don't do weak well. You like me needy, and I don't do needy well. You never once let me be the hero. I am always the rescued. You are the Helper, the Counselor, the reassuring hand upon my back when I would have sworn to you that I was the only one in the room. When I neglect you, I'm like a candle without a flame.

You don't just bring the fire. You are the fire. You cause me to jump when I want to hide. You make me to run free when I want to walk away.

Holy Spirit, don't let me ever take another step in this life without checking in with you first—and surrendering myself wholly to you.

Holy Spirit, you are welcome here. Amen.

Jennifer Dukes Lee, speaker, bestselling author,
Love Idol and *The Happiness Dare*

A Spirit-Led Heart Manifesto

A woman with a Spirit-led heart

. . . trusts that God can use her, even when her knees knock

. . . believes that when she speaks to God, he hears

. . . reaches for truth as a weapon and isn't afraid to use it

. . . tells her story, for she has walked with Jesus

. . . is not lost in the valleys or on the mountaintops

. . . fights for others, because Jesus fought for her first

. . . isn't a know-it-all, though she longs to know all there is to know

. . . doesn't have time to be distracted by drama with no eternal value

. . . believes that God loves her, and freely loves him back.

Now the Lord is the Spirit, and where the Spirit
of the Lord is, there is liberty
[emancipation from bondage, true freedom].

2 Corinthians 3:17 AMP

INTRODUCTION

Several friends meet at my home every week. We eat. We laugh. We cry. We open our Bibles and study together. One night we were reading from the book of Acts and a friend stopped me midsentence.

"I have to know," she said, "does this stuff still happen?"

The "stuff" she was talking about was believers praying for the sick. Preaching an impromptu message and people rushing to receive the good news. It was walking boldly with love and determination into a culture that didn't believe in or understand Jesus.

Our world is shifting, isn't it?

Christianity is quickly becoming a negative word in our culture rather than being perceived as the beautiful gift that it is. Sometimes our beliefs are misunderstood, criticized, and pulled apart. We realize the church isn't perfect, because it's made up of people like us. We are flawed. We are messy. We make mistakes, and we are a continual work in progress.

Despite our flaws, we have been changed by a Father's love and rescued by our Savior. Most of us desire to make a difference in our world—which is what led my friend to ask her question. She wasn't seeking to preach to a crowd of thousands. She wasn't trying to build a worldwide ministry. She asked because she longed for her faith to show up where she lived. In her home. In her workplace.

In her relationships with friends and neighbors. In her solitary moments when it's just her and God.

Wherever God desired to lead her beyond that, awesome.

Her question was a good one. Is it possible to have a Spirit-led heart today?

I believe it is, and goodness, we need it.

I may stand on a stage and speak to crowds, but I also long to speak into the hearts of the six "littles" that call me Gaga. I want them to grow up knowing that faith is impactful and God is real. I long for faith to spill onto those closest to me.

I have some big dreams, but I need God in the nitty gritty as well.

When I read my friend Jennifer Dukes Lee's powerful prayer one day on social media, I wept because it resonated. I messaged her that day (okay, that moment) and asked if we could include it in this book, for it is my heart cry. I believe it's the heart cry of many faith-filled women.

You see, we've been gifted with a Helper, but we often try to do it by ourselves.

We do more. We brainstorm more. We show up and sign up, and it works for a while because we are women and we are resourceful. After time, however, most of us burn out, get bummed out, or keep on going, running on fumes like an old car sputtering down the road. Pretty soon, there we are. Empty. Uncertain. Trying to live our faith on our own. And it just doesn't seem to match up with the hope God has placed in our hearts.

There are thousands of people and churches and nonprofits doing a beautiful work, but we need the Holy Spirit desperately, just like the early church did.

If you read my book *Come with Me: Discovering the Beauty of Following Where He Leads*, you know that I went on a journey into the book of Luke for two years. I did so because I wanted to meet Jesus all over again. I was wrestling in my faith instead of resting in it. For two years, I listened to him; I walked with him and that rough-and-tumble bunch of disciples. That journey changed me and my faith forever.

In the same way, my friend's question prompted me to take a second journey, this time into the book of Acts. The first thing we notice is a church at work. The disciples have become apostles. They are church planters and builders. They are preachers, teachers, and world changers. They aren't alone in this. They are joined by women, men, Jews, and Gentiles. There's even a rascally guy named Saul.

When we step into the book of Acts, we step into their uncertainty. They remain incredibly human and ordinary. They are dealing with a lot of challenges that currently define our own culture. Things like racism, arguing, and division. The church is growing but embattled. They face persecution and imprisonment.

Jesus had issued a startling promise to them before he left.

He promised a Helper, if they'd wait expectantly. The Helper was the Holy Spirit.

It doesn't take long to see how his presence infused life into the early church. It was power! That power had nothing to do with position or the level of education that a believer had. Instead, Jesus's followers believed that God can use anybody if he is the one who has called them. The growth of the church wasn't due to a massive platform, social media prowess, or following algorithms and insights. It was the anointing of the Holy Spirit. It couldn't be denied. It couldn't be fabricated.

This transformed the early church, and it spilled onto people nearby.

The early church wasn't always eloquent, but their words swayed thousands. They were oppressed and persecuted, but their message thrived. They received what they needed, day by day.

A Spirit-led heart still changes us today.

Do you believe that? I do.

If this promise was for the early church, then it's also for us.

Maybe you have some reservations. I get that. There are many great books written about the Holy Spirit. I've read many of them.

This book is a little different. We'll travel into the book of Acts together. Jesus introduced the Holy Spirit to the early church, and we'll listen to what Jesus had to say about him. We'll watch how the early church responded. Then we'll dig deeper into what that means for us today. We'll ask how a Spirit-led heart might lead us to live our faith and love without borders.

Living our faith and love without borders means that the Holy Spirit offers each of us a measure of confidence. We are gently empowered. We are invited to walk in truth and find direction, even if that is just the next step. We find boldness that is bigger than ourselves, yet cloaked in humility. We reach for counsel, comfort, and discernment, and it's there waiting for us. Living our faith and love without borders helps us to know why we believe and how to hold on when that feels shaky.

I long for a Spirit-led heart. I long for a Spirit-led life.

My prayer is that we'll ask the same question that my friend did, and walk away with an answer.

Is this stuff for today?

Oh, sweet friend, I believe it is.

I can't wait to see what God does when we live as if it is true.

Suzie

1

Released from Uncertainty

A Spirit-Led Heart Is Confident

A change in your perspective can allow you to embrace
a change in your position.

Lynn Cowell, *Make Your Move*

The small church was nestled along a busy highway. Inside, rafters
dipped as if in surrender. An altar, worn by tears and generations of prayers, graced the front. I was seventeen years old. I
don't remember much of what the speaker said that night. I
do recall stumbling to the altar and finding a place by myself
at the end. My tears traveled the grooves formed by those who
came before me.

I wasn't sure if I could do it.

I loved God as much as I could at this point. I'd only been a
believer for about a year, and I wasn't as spiritually savvy as those
around me. My Bible wasn't earmarked and highlighted like it is
today.

I was trying.

I showed up at church. I went to small groups. I was learning about him and what it meant to be a believer. That didn't mean I didn't have a thousand questions.

Grace seemed like a beautiful concept, but I wasn't sure how to offer it to others, much less myself. I didn't know what it meant to carry my cross. I didn't have a clue whether God could use me, because I was still trying to figure out what his love looked like.

I wept that day as I knelt at the altar because I wanted faith to be less difficult and my understanding to be greater. I wept because life was hard and I often felt isolated. I wept because I longed to know him more and to discover who I was to him.

I needed help.

As I prayed, a tap on my shoulder caused me to look up.

"It's really late," the pastor said. "You'll need to go home soon. We'll give you a ride if you need one."

I considered the face of the kind older man kneeling beside me. Not far away, his wife sat quietly on a pew.

"I just started praying," I said.

"No, honey, you've been here for a couple of hours. You've been praying intensely. We saw the Holy Spirit doing a work in you, so we waited."

As I looked around, it had to be true. The building was almost empty. Once-crowded pews held only remnants of tissues and scrawled notes.

The last thing I remembered was kneeling and whispering my request through tears.

"Can you help me?"

To this day, I can't tell you exactly what took place in those two hours, but when I stood up, I felt different. I had asked for help, and help arrived. Something miraculous began inside my hungry, hurting heart. My legs were rubbery from sitting in the same position for so long, and I stumbled to my car.

I drove home to the same old circumstances.

I was the same girl, now with swollen eyes and a cheek temporarily marked by a rugged altar, but confidence bubbled inside of me like holy water.

Nothing outwardly changed, but the Helper had arrived.

The Early Church: When Confidence Feels Wrecked

I grew into my faith and found my place in the body of Christ as a follower and believer. I discovered that God loves me even when I'm a mess. I peeled away the meaning of grace as his mercy rescued me daily. Somehow that uncertain teenager who lived in a mostly unchurched environment became a Bible teacher. A mom. A wife. A woman who longs to make a difference with her faith.

Yet there are still moments I find myself in a confidence crisis.

As I write these words, our world is in upheaval. It's turbulent, at best. People are at odds, including believers. Our world creaks with tragedy. Television and the internet flash images of mamas holding desperately to their children as they flee war-torn countries. It's almost become commonplace to hear of unexplainable and violent incidents taking place in crowded malls and subways. We live in a nation where racial wounds continue to cause pain.

There are days our confidence is shaken and it has nothing to do with the state of the world. Our confidence is shaken as we pray, yet we are unsure of when the answer is coming. Our confidence is rattled when a dream is burning inside of us, and we don't know how to take the next step—or when that dream finally arrives and it seems way too big.

Our confidence is shaken when a close relationship is struggling, or when we say the wrong thing and try to make it right. A confidence crisis the size of Texas can rattle us when a child throws three tantrums before breakfast and we want to throw our own in response.

The root of any confidence crisis is fear. Fear of failure. Fear of not being able to fix it. Fear that we aren't enough. Fear that things are never going to change. Fear of the unknown.

The early church understood fear. . . .

After the crucifixion, believers hide behind barred doors. Is it possible they celebrated a Passover meal with Jesus just days ago?

He had washed their feet. They laughed. They ate. They went deep in conversation. It was a lot like my friends and me around my own table, except for the foot-washing part.

Now everything has changed.

Judas Iscariot had led soldiers into the garden of Gethsemane to arrest Jesus. They had thought he was a friend! Peter—the guy who said he would never let Jesus down—had betrayed Jesus publicly. Soldiers now search from house to house, their swords drawn and ready. The disciples don't know whom to trust. They don't know what to do.

If we were to describe the overall morale of these believers, it would be confused and afraid. We aren't privy to their conversations, but it's not hard to imagine that they questioned whether they had heard Jesus correctly. They had thought they were building a kingdom, not preparing for a funeral. They scrutinize each other because, after all, one of their own has betrayed them. Their love for Jesus hasn't gone anywhere, but their confidence?

Wrecked.

Then one day three women trudge to a tomb. Their souls are heavy because Jesus's body rests inside. When they arrive, they are greeted by a yawning open cave and a blinding light. Two angels share the news that Jesus has risen. The women rush back to their friends to share the report.

The tomb is empty!

The disciples race to verify it for themselves. They huddle around an open tomb and examine the evidence. End of story, right? Fear conquered! All is well!

It doesn't work that way.

They go right back to their hiding hole. Still behind locked doors. Still bound in uncertainty. It would seem that an empty tomb would be enough to ease their confidence crisis, but let's put ourselves in their shoes.

This could be a trick. It could be the work of their adversaries. They want to believe, but what if they get their hopes up, only to be let down again?

Even great news seems suspicious when confidence is at an all-time low and fear is at an all-time high.

Then Jesus steps into their uncertainty.

> On the evening of that first day of the week, when the disciples were together, with the doors locked for fear of the Jewish leaders, Jesus came and stood among them and said, "Peace be with you!"
>
> John 20:19

For the next forty days, Jesus soothes and loves and challenges his followers. He strolls with two men on the road to Emmaus to ease their discouragement (Luke 24:13–32). He kneels beside Peter to remind him that he is a "rock" (Matthew 16:18). He invites Thomas to put fingers in his wounds to relieve his doubt (John 20:27).

Can you imagine the deep breath they all took? Everything is right again. Jesus is back at the helm, right where he belongs. The world is moving in the right direction once again . . . until Jesus drops this truth bomb on them.

You are now the church.

He tells them to take everything he's taught them and live it. He tells them they'll share the gospel at home and far away. He tells them that he has confidence in them, but he has to go away.

Wait.

No, Jesus.

If the root of a confidence crisis is fear, this root goes as deep as the ocean. Following Jesus was never easy, but Jesus led the way. If they had a question, they knew where to go. If a problem seemed too big to solve, they put it in his lap. Sure, he challenged them, but it's a lot easier to jump out of an airplane tandem than it is to jump solo.

Um, Jesus. I was the one who blew it. Are you sure you got the right person here?

I've witnessed your miracles, Jesus, but I'm not you.
What if I mess this up?

That third question is a familiar one for me. Our natural reaction to fear is doubt, and the longer it lingers the more it hinders. It can cause us to run the other direction when Jesus has so much more for us. We may choose inaction over doing it badly or falling on our face. We tell the world that God has a plan for us, but doubt it privately. This is where we might lose our way. We are so busy mulling over our fears or doubts that we fail to understand that God sees it differently.

The longer doubt lingers, the more it hinders.

Jesus had shown his followers how to pray. He taught them how to love people. They stood next to him as lepers were healed, demons were cast out, and people condemned for their sins were restored. While they loiter in doubt, Jesus is already envisioning the eternal mark his believers will leave on the world.

Many times our confidence is waylaid by doubt when our Savior is cheering us on, already seeing us cross the finish line.

Fear clouds vision, but faith shows us the next step. Even as our human imperfections tend to march front and center, God places his trust in us. None of our doubts disqualify his belief in us. He is asking not for perfection, but for a partnership.

These truths are displayed as Jesus remains with his followers for forty days.

When it's time for him to return to the Father, the promise he made earlier is their anchor.

> And now I will send the Holy Spirit, just as my Father promised. But stay here in the city *until the Holy Spirit comes and fills you with power* from heaven.
>
> Luke 24:49 NLT

Jesus places his hands on them and blesses them. In the midst of that oh-so-personal moment, Jesus is taken into heaven. The disciples can't help but praise God, with wonder on their faces and in their hearts.

Did they totally understand the promise?

Not yet, but they believed that what he spoke was true, and that was enough.

Your Promise: You Are Loved, Rescued, and Empowered

The Holy Spirit is introduced in Genesis 1:2 and weaves throughout Scripture. Jesus introduces him in a fresh new way to the early church. The Holy Spirit had been *with* God's people for generations, but now he will be *in* them.

Jesus instructed the disciples to "go" in the name of the Father, Son, and Holy Spirit (Matthew 28:19). The Holy Spirit isn't elevated above the Father or the Son, nor beneath, but seen as coming alongside. He plays a specific role in our faith. Martyn Lloyd-Jones, a theologian and teacher, described the Holy Spirit's role this way:

> The Father is all the fulness of the Godhead invisible, without form, 'whom no man hath seen, nor can see' (1 Tim. 6:16); that is the Father. The Son is all the fulness of the Godhead manifested visibly, 'For in him dwelleth all the fulness of the Godhead bodily' (Col. 2:9); that is the Son. . . . And the Spirit is all the fulness of the Godhead acting immediately upon the creature.[1]

Maybe like me, the first time you read this, you had to go back and reread it. May I simplify it?

- We were created, and we are loved by our heavenly Father.
- We were rescued by our Savior.
- We are empowered to live our faith through the Holy Spirit.

Let's take this a little deeper:

- Our heavenly Father is invisible to the naked eye, though his love is vast.
- The Son of God made the Father's love visible to a desperate world.
- The Holy Spirit helps us live our salvation so that a lost world sees God more clearly.

Isn't that beautiful? This is our faith! The Trinity reveals how God loves, seeks, and helps us in every part of our relationship with him. The Holy Spirit is often referred to as the Helper. He ignites our faith. He understands the heart of the Father over us.

When we talk about the Holy Spirit, we often refer to him as "it." The Holy Spirit is more than a feeling, a gift, or an influence. He's not limited to his gifts.

Can we just be honest about the fact that we sometimes shy away from the Holy Spirit? We may be so unsure of his role (or that he exists) that we eliminate him from our faithview altogether. Is it possible that we've overlooked or discounted this stunning promise made by Jesus himself?

Let's crack open our faithview to include this truth.

We are loved by the Father and saved by the Son, and we have a Helper—right now, always, in every situation.

How exciting is that?

Your Invitation: Integrate the Holy Spirit into Your Faithview

Fear is the root of most confidence crises, but our faith is the target. Our faith in God. Faith in who we are to him. Faith that trusts that he is sovereign, and at work even when we don't see it. Faith that we might have a role to play in changing the world.

I stumbled upon a conversational thread in a social media post not too long ago. Years ago, my husband, Richard, and I opened our home to college students. We played marathon games of Nertz and ate a ton of chicken enchiladas. We loved each student, which is why my heart sank as I read the conversation. It was from one of those individuals, now a young father and husband.

Our friend: *I don't know about my faith anymore.*
A stranger: *Me either.*
Our friend: *Man, I look around and I'm not sure that the church is relevant.*
Another stranger: *Yeah, they are all after something.*

The conversation spiraled.

Words heaped upon words. Some of those commenting hadn't experienced Christ, but they were happy to share their opinions on Christianity. Some had once attended church, but they walked away disillusioned with organized religion. Some comments were reactionary and volatile. Many were painfully honest, rife with longing.

My heart hurt, but I know that it's important to give space to anyone (ourselves included) asking hard questions about faith. Social media might not seem like sacred space, but in this instance, it's where our friend's search landed. As I listened in on this conversation, his faith crisis hit me in the feelers too. I wandered back to those beautiful, fun, messy moments. I remembered the times we knelt with college students, much like that pastor knelt beside me when I was weeping at the altar. I thought about those crazy Nertz games and baking mass quantities of food. We laughed a lot. We held long conversations about faith. We listened when they shared their mistakes and sins, and held them close as we walked into Jesus's love. We piled in airplanes to travel to poverty-torn nations to build churches and share the gospel. It was hard work, but we loved it.

Though fear is the root of most confidence crises, our faith is the target.

When someone we care about is questioning their faith or saying that the church is no longer viable, it can rattle us. It might make us wonder whether we did something wrong. It might make us itch to fix something or someone and make it all right again. We might wonder if our efforts were in vain. We can get drawn into the conversation in a negative way as we try to make them see it our way. All of these responses are human, but they take our eyes off the true battleground.

- The truth is that we have an enemy who desires to distort faith, and he is hard at work.
- The truth is that the church is made up of people, and that can be messy.
- The truth is that we are only asked to do the best we know as a parent, as a friend, or in ministry, and we don't get to stake a claim in a person's personal relationship with God, no matter what that looks like.

My friend needed to ask his questions, and those questions didn't nullify who God is. The real battleground in that conversation was my friend's faith.

He was in a confidence crisis.

Jesus reminded the disciples to be direct with God when they needed help. That's just as true when someone we care about is in a confidence crisis.

Don't bargain with God. Be direct. Ask for what you need. This is not a cat-and-mouse, hide-and-seek game we're in. If your little boy asks for a serving of fish, do you scare him with a live snake on his plate? If your little girl asks for an egg, do you trick her with a spider? As bad as you are, you wouldn't think of such a thing—you're at least decent to your own children. And don't you think the Father who conceived you in love will *give the Holy Spirit when you ask him*?

Luke 11:10–13 MESSAGE

It wasn't my job to make it all go away. I'm not big enough, and it's not what he was asking for. Instead of letting my emotions dictate, I asked the Holy Spirit for help.

For him.

For those who were commenting.

For me, as the enemy tried to erode my confidence in the ministry we had been so privileged to partner in.

Are you in a confidence crisis as a loved one struggles with faith? Let's pause and ask the Father to send the Holy Spirit to help. The good news is that he's right there, inside of you already. You don't have to carry this burden alone.

Father, I need help. Thank you for the gift of the Holy Spirit, who helps me do what you've asked me to do. Who shows me what is mine to address and what to place in your hands. You are a good Father, and you give good gifts—and I receive this gift. Thank you for renewed confidence in this area, not in the circumstance or even in what I can or cannot do, but in your love for this one.

Don't be afraid to ask the Holy Spirit to show you what you might not see. Ask for guidance. Ask him to speak to that person in ways that he or she will understand. If you feel him leading you to act or say something, write that down. Pray for direction and wisdom as you follow that leading.

Write down this person's name. Write down today's date, for you are releasing him or her to God's capable hands. Write down anything you sense the Holy Spirit whispering inside of you. That's not saying you are giving up or don't care, but that you are partnering with God in all your next steps.

We can be assured of this as we battle for a loved one.

- God loves them.
- Jesus waits to rescue them.
- The Holy Spirit will show them the way home.

So what about my friend?

I did exactly what I just asked you to do. I asked for help. I sensed that I was supposed to let him know that I care. I sent a private message saying that I believed in him and that I was available, if needed. Then it was his turn, if he so desired.

We talked briefly. I gave him room to share some of the hard questions he was asking. It wasn't my job to resolve his doubt, for that is the work of the Holy Spirit. My role was to let him know that Richard and I were available as sounding boards.

It wasn't my job to fix his confidence crisis, but I could pray. I could respond to his questions with truth and gentleness. The rest was up to the Holy Spirit. Just as he lives in me, he lives in my friend. He sees the scope of the battle. He sees what I do not. He knows that God loves him more than I ever could and is reaching for him.

Several weeks later, my old friend sent a message.

"I'm finding my way back," he said.

His faith is in the process of restoration. He is moving away from defining faith by people or a tradition or a doctrine. He is placing his trust in a God who loves him and a Savior who rescued him rather than defining his faith by politics or the actions of a handful of work-in-progress individuals—or even by his doubts. His standard is Christ. The Holy Spirit is helping him rediscover what faith looks like, and how to live it intimately.

If your confidence crisis is wrapped around a loved one's decisions or a loss of faith, it's likely rooted in fear. The Helper eases into that confidence crisis to remind you of what you can and cannot do on your own. He frees you to bring that loved one to our heavenly Father in prayer. He releases the need to control the outcome, allowing you instead to be open to play a part as the Holy Spirit leads, or to trust as God works behind the scenes.

Someone else's confidence crisis can have the power to drain life from our faith. We become so busy trying to repair, foster, and manage what is beyond our ability that we live in defeat or continual frustration. But God's plan for that person does not hinge on your efforts.

And if the Spirit of him who raised Jesus from the dead is living in you, he who raised Christ from the dead will also give life to your mortal bodies *because of his Spirit who lives in you.*

Romans 8:11

It's based on what has already been done on the cross.

Your faith is not limited by your friend's struggle, but rather, your faith is empowered as you invite the Holy Spirit into *your* confidence crisis. When you ask the Holy Spirit to join you, confidence swings to the truth that God loves that person and is at work.

What if it's you asking the hard questions?

You may feel shut down or guilty for having uncertainties about your faith. Your doubts don't turn God away. You don't have to be afraid to say how you feel, because he already knows. As you ask him to meet you in your confidence crisis, the Holy Spirit will remind you of who you are (Romans 8:16).

We all have doubts. Every one of us, even that woman sitting in the pew across from you who seems to have it all together struggles with confidence.

A couple of years ago I received a message from a reader through my blog. She was a praying, in-love-with-Jesus believer. She was also in a confidence crisis. I had written a twenty-one-day series about moving past what you cannot change. That day I expressed that we all doubt from time to time.

She responded that when she felt doubt, she also felt shame. This made her more frustrated, because someone once told her that Christians don't have confidence issues. It only made her doubt herself more.

I was thankful that she bravely asked her question, but it made my heart heavy. If doubting makes you a "bad Christian," then that disqualifies most of us, including many great biblical women and men of faith. When the Lord spoke to Moses and spelled out his plan for him (Exodus 3:1–12), Moses's knees started knocking. He didn't feel like the right guy for the job, and he told God that he stuttered (Exodus 4:10–11). Even as God expressed confidence, Moses pointed out his own inadequacies. His greatest, he said, was that he stuttered. For a long time, I thought Moses's stuttering was literal—until I read this verse:

> Moses was educated in all the wisdom of the Egyptians and was powerful in speech and action.
>
> Acts 7:22

When we study further, we discover that Moses was educated by the best of the best. He lived as an adoptive grandson of Pharaoh. Everyone, including God, recognized Moses as a born leader long before he stood at the burning bush.

We know the end of the story. Moses went on to lead a nation. He parted the Red Sea with his staff. He led an army across dry ground. Biblical history labels him one of the greatest leaders ever.

The root of his confidence crisis was fear, but the target was his faith.

There are other examples of confidence crises. Paul the apostle was passionate about sharing the good news, but he was criticized for his public speaking. That critical word from listeners had the power to plant doubt and make him give up. Can you imagine speaking to a crowd, only to hear feedback that you are "unimpressive" and your speaking "amounts to nothing" (2 Corinthians 10:10)?

Ouch! Ouch! Ouch!

Thank you very much. Exit stage right. I'm never coming back again!

Yet Paul planted churches. He witnessed miracles and was instrumental in many of them. He is considered the greatest evangelist of all time. God used him to spread the church to the Gentile nations. Maybe he wasn't the best speaker, but he was anointed, and that was better than a perfect three-point sermon.

As we follow Jesus, we won't have a doubt-free walk. Our Spirit-led heart will lead us to a dependent walk instead. The woman who so courageously sent her question was not a "bad" Christian, but rather an ordinary Christ follower like most of us. As we follow Jesus, we will see how human we are. It will lead either to comparison or to placing our confidence in him. When we stop gazing at our own inadequacies, we are free to celebrate that God uses us despite them.

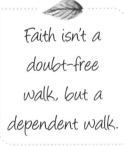

Faith isn't a doubt-free walk, but a dependent walk.

Consider your doubt in a whole new way.

Yes, you doubted, but you believed.

Yes, you doubted, but you asked the Holy Spirit to step into those doubts.

Yes, you doubted, but you acted anyway.

That's faith! Instead of beating ourselves up over doubts, let's throw our hands in the air and rejoice that faith leads ordinary people like you and me to be used in powerful ways—because our confidence is established in him.

Spirit-Led Confidence without Borders

The promise arrived just as Jesus said it would (Acts 2:1–4).

About 120 Jesus followers were in the upper room. They had prayed for ten days. Suddenly a wind blew through and tongues of fire settled on each person. Their voices rose like thunder, carrying to the streets below, where thousands observed the Day of Pentecost, a major religious festival held fifty days after Passover.

The people in the street stopped what they were doing. They gazed at the upper room.

Utterly amazed, they asked: "Aren't all these who are speaking Galileans? Then how is it that each of us hears them in our native language? Parthians, Medes and Elamites; residents of Mesopotamia, Judea and Cappadocia, Pontus and Asia, Phrygia and Pamphylia, Egypt and the parts of Libya near Cyrene; visitors from Rome (both Jews and converts to Judaism); Cretans and Arabs—we hear them declaring the wonders of God in our own tongues!" Amazed and perplexed, they asked one another, "What does this mean?"

Acts 2:7–12

The 120 in the upper room were speaking in different languages, but it's their message that captured attention. These same believers were trapped in fear just a few weeks earlier. They trembled at Jesus's instruction to go into the world. Now they shouted at the top of their voices about God's goodness.

Their circumstances hadn't changed, but their faith was empowered.

Their confidence crisis shifted from fear to faith. Their attention was squarely on what was possible, rather than tangled in doubt over the future.

This is Spirit-led confidence without borders. We aren't blind. We see what is happening in the world. We know what we are facing. We understand the obstacles. Fear or uncertainty should be our cry; instead, our confidence is in God's goodness. It spills out in our message. It pours over our everyday life. His goodness is written into our worldview. We are assured that we have a role to play—as a friend, as a single woman or single mom, as a wife, as a grandmother, as a daughter of a Most High God. We stand shoulder to shoulder with other ordinary women of faith, and our hearts and lives reflect his goodness.

The Holy Spirit activates our confidence in God rather than in ourselves or in our circumstances. We spill that news of goodness in our homes. In our nation. In our relationships. In our churches. Across the world.

I sometimes look back at my seventeen-year-old self who knelt at an altar, so desperate for help. I was hemmed in. My borders were my home life. My lack of knowledge. My age. It felt like I'd never get there, wherever "there" might be. I asked for help, and help arrived. The physical evidence of that night was a stack of tear-saturated tissues, but the spiritual evidence remains within me today.

I didn't know what I needed, but God did. I didn't have a clue where to find confidence, but it was right inside of me all along. The borders were real, but God broke them one by one.

Spirit-led confidence impacts the world.

Sometimes the people you influence live across the street. Sometimes that growing confidence spills onto the child sitting at your feet.

Sometimes it's the woman looking back at you in the mirror.

The Word

And I will ask the Father, and he will give you another advocate to help you and be with you forever—the Spirit of truth. The world cannot accept him, because it neither sees him nor knows him. But you know him, for he lives with you and will be *in* you.

JOHN 14:16–17

Your Spirit-Led Promise

God loves you.
Jesus rescued you.
The Holy Spirit helps you.

Your Spirit-Led Invitation

Welcome the Holy Spirit into your faithview.

Prayer

Jesus, you promised a Helper and I need help. Thank you for offering this gift to help me live my faith. I open my heart and my life to the truth that this gift is for me. Amen.

2

Power Greater Than Our Own

A Spirit-Led Heart Is
Empowered

An encounter with Jesus was an encounter with God
for the disciples. In the same way an encounter with
the Holy Spirit is an encounter with God for you.

Henry Blackaby, *Experiencing God*

Two-year-old Josiah was transitioning from his crib to a big-boy
bed. Keeping him in it was a nightly effort. His mom and dad
left the crib in his room for those nights when they were too exhausted to get up several times to put him back into his new bed.
One night they were on a date, and I was watching Josiah and his
older brother. Josiah had climbed out of bed several times and run
downstairs too many times to count. I finally put him in the crib.
Thump.
Thump.
Thump.

I tried to ignore the sounds, but they didn't stop, so I trudged back upstairs. I shone my smartphone light into the room and gasped at the sight before me. Josiah stood on the edge of the crib, his toes gripping the rail. His face was covered with his blue blankie. He held his arms out like a bird in flight.

I ran toward him just as he jumped off the edge of his crib into his new toddler bed.

Thump.

He missed the ceiling fan by less than an inch.

He pulled the blanket off his head and giggled in delight.

That's when he saw me. His smile was wide, as if to say, "Did you see that?" I gathered my grandson in my arms and gently scolded him. We piled in the rocking chair and I held him close. Within a few minutes his breathing slowed and my little guy finally fell asleep in my arms.

Josiah is an adventurer.

He walked early. He ran early. He climbs anything that can be climbed. He's athletic, surprisingly so for such a little guy. He looks for edges and high places, for that's where he is comfortable. He has a temper that flares like dynamite, though he's sorry immediately. He's tenderhearted and loves making people laugh.

Josiah is named after a king (2 Kings 22) who was eight years old when he inherited his father's corrupt kingdom. King Josiah reigned in Jerusalem for thirty-one years. His love for God was so strong that he banished idolatry, and he eventually turned around generations of abuse and evil.

Our Josiah came to our family through adoption. His name has significant meaning, and that will be his story to tell one day. When he was born, my husband and I were outside the room. He struggled to take his first breath. My daughter sent me a text.

Please pray, Mom.

We prayed.

The doctor and a flurry of nurses pounded on him until he finally sucked in enough air to let out a shriek. Josiah was on the scene! He came into the world loved and marked by God. I don't know what his exact purpose will be. The fact that he's willing to stand on the edge of a crib with a blanket over his head and fly . . . that's going to somehow play into it. Those characteristics of adventure and fearlessness will be mighty tools in God's hands.

My prayer is that he'll be empowered to change the world, just as young King Josiah did.

Our job is to keep him safe in the meantime.

The Early Church: Power for a Purpose

The Greek word for Holy Spirit power is *dynamis*, which is related to our English word *dynamite*. This isn't a small amount of power. It shakes up and tears down. It breaks down barriers.

I was at a family gathering a few years ago. The location was down a winding road, settled among hills, caves, towering trees, and winding creek beds. In the middle of our celebration, one of the guests pulled out a small cylinder.

"What's that?" I asked.

"Dynamite," he said.

Whoa.

I had never seen dynamite up close, and I wasn't that excited to see it now. He and some of the other men went behind a barn to light the small stick of dynamite. I remained at a distance. I questioned whether this was a good idea. Someone standing close shrugged off my question as overprotective. He told me that the guy lighting the dynamite was familiar with it.

It didn't reassure me. This was *dynamite*.

When the small stick of dynamite exploded, bystanders covered their ears. Some ran. Others whooped and hollered. Since no one was hurt, they labeled the explosion a success.

While I'm thankful no one was hurt, dynamite is no plaything. It has the power to hurt a lot of people if things go wrong.

If you've ever been abused by someone in religious power, the fact that the Holy Spirit is described as dynamite may turn you away. The last thing you want is someone else's power robbing you of yours. You don't want to be overpowered by their personality or plans. You don't want to be hit by spiritual shrapnel when someone abuses that power. Thank goodness *dynamis* power is nothing like that. It doesn't knock someone down so that another person can rise higher. It's not abusive.

Instead, it is power that ignites from within. It is power that is greater than our own. Jesus described it as being "clothed with power from on high" (Luke 24:49).

Dynamis power was displayed when Jesus touched or prayed with people. It was often described as power emanating from him, like when the woman with the issue of blood was healed (Luke 8:43–48). *Dynamis* power showed up in Jesus's actions and also his words as he sent demons running to the hillside (Luke 8:26–39). Jesus told the disciples to wait for the Holy Spirit. They emerged from the upper room with *dynamis* power flowing through their spiritual veins.

Fast-forward thirty years.

In Acts 3, Peter and John are on the way to the temple to teach. A man is being carried by family members to the main gate. He has been lame since birth. Begging for alms is his only means of survival. As the apostles approach, the lame man asks for money.

> Peter looked straight at him, as did John. Then Peter said, "Look at us!" So the man gave them his attention, expecting to get something from them. Then Peter said, "Silver or gold I do not have, but what I do have I give you. In the name of Jesus Christ of Nazareth, walk."
>
> Acts 3:4–6

The beggar is miraculously healed. He leaps to his feet! There is nothing the apostles could have given the man on their own, but that's what is so beautiful about this story.

This is *dynamis* power in action.

It's greater than Peter or John. It's greater than what the man expects to receive. The crowd is so inspired by this miracle and

Peter's ensuing message that the number of believers swells to five thousand, not including women or children.

This is power for a purpose. A man is healed, but a city is awakened.

What I love most about this story is the timeline. Peter and John are thirty years older than they were when they received this power. It's as fresh now as it was then. They are now leaders, but their power source is the Holy Spirit within. *Dynamis* power fuels the faith of the apostles. It empowers the faith of the family members who carry a lame man to the gate. It triggers the prayer that heals his legs. It stuns a crowd who believes a coin is the best (or only) option for a hungry, despairing man.

The Holy Spirit empowers for a purpose.

This scene would make a great ending for a movie, if not for what happens next. The healing is good news to everybody except those in charge. They seize Peter and John and arrest them. Because it's late in the day, the courts are closed. Peter and John have to remain in jail overnight. The next day, rulers, elders, and teachers of the law meet to talk about these two crazy troublemakers. They haul them out of jail and demand to know by what power the lame man was healed.

> *Then Peter, filled with the Holy Spirit*, said to them: "Rulers and elders of the people! If we are being called to account today for an act of kindness shown to a man who was lame and are being asked how he was healed, then know this, you and all the people of Israel: It is by the name of Jesus Christ of Nazareth, whom you crucified but whom God raised from the dead, that this man stands before you healed. Jesus is 'the stone you builders rejected, which has become the cornerstone.'"
>
> Acts 4:8–11

Imagine sitting in a dungeon-like cell all night long. Imagine that you did nothing wrong. Imagine that your faith-filled response freed a man from a lifetime of poverty and pain. Imagine that the people standing before you have the power to throw you in jail.

Peter and John should have been intimidated.

They should have been discouraged. They should have been dismayed by the authorities' attempts to stop their good works.

Dynamis power shatters the "shoulds" in this story.

Instead, Peter is filled with the Holy Spirit and speaks to the authorities. This word *filled* describes immediate, sudden inspiration. Peter is given wisdom, courage, and the words needed at the time. As he speaks, the religious rulers can't help but notice that a couple of former fishermen are trumping earthly, abusive power with uncanny humility and wisdom.

> When they saw the courage of Peter and John and realized that they were unschooled, ordinary men, *they were astonished and they took note that these men had been with Jesus.*
>
> Acts 4:13

Let's stay here just for a moment. I don't want us to rush past this remarkable statement.

The apostles are marked by their relationship with Jesus.

This is the purpose. It's what *dynamis* power does. It's what it did for Peter and John, and it's what it does in us. This power points to Jesus. It's the opposite of what earthly power does, because we are not front and center.

The needs that are on our Father's heart are front and center.

God's love for the world is front and center.

When the religious rulers and authority look at these Jesus followers, they see him in them. They comprehend power that comes through position, but this power? They don't grasp it at all.

They resort to threats, warning Peter and John to never publicly speak the name of Jesus again.

It's almost laughable.

These followers of Christ have been at this for thirty years. Their pattern is as familiar as the sun rising. They will follow the call on their lives to share and live the gospel, no matter where that leads. The apostles leave the presence of the authorities and immediately begin to seek the presence of God. This leads to one of the most powerful prayers recorded in Scripture:

> "Now, Lord, consider their threats and enable your servants to speak your word with great boldness. Stretch out your hand to heal and perform signs and wonders through the name of your holy servant Jesus." After they prayed, the place where they were meeting was shaken. *And they were all filled with the Holy Spirit* and spoke the word of God boldly.
>
> Acts 4:29–31

When the disciples finish praying, they are filled with the Holy Spirit.

Unlike in the upper room, there is no wind or tongues of fire. Yet the Holy Spirit makes himself known. The house is shaken. They are filled and immediately begin to speak boldly, despite the threats just levied against them.

Your Promise: You Are Filled and Refilled

The apostles prayed and were filled. The word *filled* might seem confusing. After all, the disciples were already filled with the Holy Spirit. Acts 4:31 describes them as being filled again. We find this in several instances throughout Scripture. For example, the disciples walk away from a difficult ministry trip, and they are filled with the Holy Spirit (Acts 13:52). There are times that they pray and are filled with the Holy Spirit.

The word *fill* seems like a one-time event, yet we fill ourselves continually with a lot of things. We fill ourselves with food, and then we eat again a few hours later. We fill our calendars and lives with activities, knowing that next month we'll do the same.

Some of the things we fill ourselves with have value, others not as much.

What if we are filled with the Holy Spirit over and over again?

Different from an earthly filling, the Source is within. It's an abundance of the Holy Spirit as we offer our life as a spiritual receptacle.

We are consistently emptied as we live our faith. We are consistently filled as we live our faith. Paul reminds the church in Ephesians 5:18, "Do not get drunk on wine, which leads to debauchery. Instead, be filled with the Spirit." We tend to place the emphasis on the wine or drunkenness in this passage and miss the promise. The Holy Spirit is not a one-time encounter.

We reach for the Holy Spirit when we feel overwhelmed, small, or overpowered—and we are filled.

We reach for the Holy Spirit when we are hurt—and we are filled.

We reach for the Holy Spirit when life isn't working out the way we think it should—and we are filled.

We reach for the Holy Spirit when we've poured out and poured out—and we are filled.

A Spirit-led heart goes through a continual process of emptying and refilling. When Peter and John prayed their prayer (along with other believers), they were reaching for all that Jesus promised.

Let's break down that prayer and discover how this plays out in our own lives.

Lord, consider their threats.

The apostles faced real threats. I've experienced the rare instance when someone threatened me, and it's sobering. This was the apostles' constant reality. What threat are you facing? When you encounter obstacles, it's okay to acknowledge they are real.

- *Lord, my marriage is threatened.*
- *Father, my physical body is under siege.*
- *I'm doing all I know to do, and nothing's working.*
- *Jesus, I love you, but it's been a long time since I felt you. I feel like my faith is in a war zone.*

God doesn't balk at our honesty. We don't have to pretend that things are easier than they are. We don't have to fake it until we make it. While we see these obstacles with natural eyes, the Holy Spirit links those events with God's plan. The power we need is within us.

We are *filled* as Jesus followers.

What does that look like? It might be an appropriate or Holy Spirit–led response at the right moment. It is patience when ours is thin. It's wisdom that allows our brain to catch up with our emotions, so that we can deal with the real problem rather than create more. It is faith in an impossible situation. A Spirit-led, empowered heart believes that his power is greater than a right-now situation and right-now feelings.

Lord, consider their threats.

We are honest about the threat. We are honest about how challenging it is. We know where our strength comes from and where to turn.

We have a Helper. The threat is real, but so is our God.

Give us boldness.

If someone threatens to ruin your life if you speak the name of Jesus, it's going to give you pause. The apostles knew there was a price to pay if they disobeyed. As they spoke this prayer, it was with the knowledge that there would be consequences.

The warning was real, but so was the call on the apostles' lives.

Sometimes our struggle is a lack of faith, or trusting God. More often, it's having the boldness to do what he asks. A synonym for boldness is *chutzpah*. It's a word that means cheekiness. It is sometimes used in a negative sense, but in this instance, it means fearlessness. Fearlessness to do what Jesus asks, even when we know there's a price to pay. Fearlessness to trust that he'll show us what to do. Fearlessness to obey God regardless of the enemy's lies.

We are aware of the threat.

Fearless doesn't mean that we aren't afraid, but that fear holds less power than the joy of following a path God has carved out for us brings.

Perform miracles and wonders in the name of Jesus.

If the religious leaders thought they'd silence the apostles, they were sorely misinformed. If you've ever witnessed an unexpected and undeserved miracle, you can't help but tell someone about it.

Peter and John weren't trying to impress a soul. They just wanted to be a mouthpiece for the gospel. Jesus saved them. He believed in them. He was the Son of God, the long-awaited Messiah. They witnessed Jesus performing miracles. Jesus often challenged them during those miracles, asking them to believe in the impossible.

I've heard many Bible-believing Christians say that miracles no longer exist. Yet how do we explain away those that occur?

We may fear asking for a miracle, that we'll look foolish if it doesn't happen the way we think it will. I believe one day we'll look back and see those scenes play out differently. We'll see miracles that dominoed for generations. We'll see miracles we took for granted. We'll look back and see a specific request denied so that a miracle with a greater eternal outcome might unfold.

Miracles reflect the Miracle Worker.

While I've not seen the Red Sea part or a dead man burst from a tomb, I know that miracles do take place. I experienced one myself nearly a quarter of a century ago. I've rarely talked about it, and those close to me have asked why. The purpose of that miracle wasn't to wrap a ministry around it. God had one person on his heart. She didn't believe in God. As a personal witness to that miracle, she confessed that there is something to this thing called faith.

It was *dynamis* power with a purpose.

My friend Jim believes in miracles. He believes that when he prays, God listens. One day he was in a coffee shop. He was introduced to a stranger by a mutual friend. As they chatted, the man explained what was going on in his family at the time. Jim gently placed his hand on the man's shoulder and said something like, "God, we need a miracle. And while you are at it, will you reveal your purpose in this?"

It was a spontaneous, drive-by prayer. It wasn't showy. It didn't draw attention to Jim, but it drew spiritual attention to the need.

It's as natural as breathing to him. If there's a need, then he's going to go to God right then. He doesn't define the miracle, but he expects something to happen.

What if we start living the same way?

We live with expectancy. We don't know the details or how it will play out. We simply ask God to show up and anticipate that he will. We believe that a miracle shines a light on our faith and on the truth that God lives. We are prepared to be a part of the miracle, if that's what God wants, but we don't look for a lead role.

Our natural inclination is to fret. We talk about the problem, person, or situation until we tie ourselves in worry. Those emotions are valid, yet we have help in the midst of them. There may be a miracle waiting, or even unfolding, that we cannot see.

Another inclination is to ignore miracles altogether until we desperately need one ourselves. At that point, we turn to God out of desperation rather than belief.

Catherine Marshall said the Holy Spirit "insists on taking us into the realm of the miraculous."[1]

Let's take him up on that invitation.

Ask the Holy Spirit to help you believe. To notice that one who needs prayer over your pity. To turn to him daily, so that when you need a miracle, that prayer is as natural as breathing. That miracles and wonders, no matter what they look like, will draw an unbelieving world to Christ.

Your Invitation: Reveal You Have Been with Jesus

I collect stories like some might collect precious stones.

These are only a few of them.

She was in jail and addicted, but she accepted God's love. Today she is a chaplain in the same prison where she was once bound. She recaptured the love of her grown children. She's the woman you see at the front of the church dancing in joy.

It's not hard to see that she has been with Jesus.

She was religious. Bored. Wondering why a God so big didn't take up much room in her life. She stepped out of tradition and into faith that challenged and astounded her. Not everyone understands her newfound excitement, but she can't wait to see what is ahead. Though she has studied the Bible for years, it now feels like a love letter.

It's not hard to see that she has been with Jesus!

She was the one they looked up to, but was secretly having an affair. She tired of her secret sin and the shame it brought. She confessed to her husband and to God. Today she shares her story freely. In the beginning, it was painful and she was often criticized, but she presses on. Her greatest hope is to reach women scarred by sin and show them what real love looks like.

When she kneels with sin-trapped women, they can't help but see that she has been with Jesus.

She was shy. Uncertain. She felt called to minister to women even though that seemed ridiculous. She trusted God and obeyed. Today she speaks to women across the globe and delights that God knew her well, even when she couldn't see it the same way.

Oh, the miracle of a life touched by Jesus!

When we ask to walk in the *dynamis* power of the Holy Spirit, we become witnesses of what God can do.

We begin to reflect him. His love. His eternal perspective over our limited earthly view. We reflect his touch in the broken places.

We were supposed to act one way. We were told who we were and to live within the margins of what we can do. But we opened our hearts to *dynamis* power and embraced our identity as a child of God.

This might feel intimidating to you, because we make mistakes. We stumble. We might not wake up feeling like a world changer. Our *dynamis* stories may have begun decades ago or are as fresh as this morning. It's not limited to a single moment or event, but played out repeatedly as we are filled with that power.

We are filled, and we empty out, so we hold up our lives like empty cisterns for a refill. *Dynamis* power isn't reserved for healing the lame or standing in front of a group of abusive leaders. It's ours to request as our feet hit the floor in the morning. It's ours to reach for when our kids are on our last nerve. It's for that impossible situation or that flash of anger or anxiousness that tries to take you down a road you don't want to travel.

Just as I collect women's stories that reflect Jesus, I want to be careful to gather them in my own life. For these are often the miracles I tend to miss. If I look at the daily miracles, they look like this:

I was angry, but empowered to respond wisely.

I was hurt, but empowered as peace seeped over the source of my pain.

I felt unsure what to do, but was empowered one small step at a time.

I was guilty of losing my temper, but empowered as I accepted mercy and a fresh start.

A Spirit-led, empowered heart

- is honest about the challenge
- is unafraid to ask for help
- notices miracles great and small
- celebrates what only God can do

Have you taken the time to celebrate your *dynamis* story?

It might be your overarching story. You were addicted and now you are free. You were abandoned, but you found love and security in Christ. You were lost, and now you are found. It might be your right-now story.

Don't go one more moment without rejoicing in that miracle.

I was .... ,

but I was empowered and ....

Perhaps your story is unfolding and you aren't sure what to celebrate. This is your promise. You are empowered by the Holy Spirit despite that harsh word spoken over you. You are empowered

49

despite that mountain in your marriage or in that relationship. You are empowered as you ask for help. You are empowered by the Holy Spirit, who is in you.

Ask to be filled.

Refuse to run on empty or in your own grit-your-teeth strength.

When you wake up, reach for the promise of a Spirit-led, empowered life, believing that it's for you and for today. When you fail (because we all do), go to the Source. Talk to God about that very real hurdle you keep running into. Stop and celebrate every time he fills you and you grow through a situation.

His *dynamis* power within you is greater than your own, and that's worth celebrating, even as this new chapter is being written.

Spirit-Led Empowerment without Borders

Peter and John could have tossed the man a coin and gone on their way. If they didn't have it on them, they could have found one. They gave him something greater. *Dynamis* power leaped from their prayers to his need, and that altered not only his body, but the trajectory of his life.

> I pray that out of his glorious riches he may strengthen you with *power through his Spirit in your inner being*, so that Christ may dwell in your hearts through faith.
>
> Ephesians 3:16–17

This power is the same word used when the house was shaken as Peter and John prayed.

A Spirit-led, empowered heart is shaken.

We are filled, and *dynamis* power starts shaking us up. It shakes up our homes. It shakes up our closest relationships. It shakes up our ministries and our jobs and our nonprofit endeavors. It shakes up our churches. It shakes our faith that has gone stagnant.

If we are praying for a Spirit-led, empowered heart, let's not stop there.

Let's ask him to shake up those thoughts that have held us captive for far too long. While you are at it, Holy Spirit, shake up our preconceptions. Shake up our limited view of who God is and what he can do. Shake our apathy. Shake the boundaries we've placed on our faith.

When we are filled daily, we become a conduit for a miracle. Our faith becomes a testimony that Jesus is more than a good story.

When people meet us, they won't see perfection, because that's not what an empowered, Spirit-led heart looks like. They aren't intimidated by our credentials. They may even see that we are works in progress.

But they'll see that we've been with Jesus.

Like my sweet adventurer Josiah, there we are, standing on the edge of our faith. We hold out our arms as we step out, knowing that Jesus meets us there.

The Word

We are witnesses of these things and so is the Holy Spirit, who is given by God to those who obey him.

ACTS 5:32 NLT

Your Spirit-Led Promise

Dynamis power reflects that you have been with Jesus.

Your Spirit-Led Invitation

Be filled (and refilled) with power for a purpose.

Prayer

Jesus, I sometimes run on empty. I try to do things on my own. I leave you out of the equation. I open my heart to your dynamis power today, tomorrow, and all my days. As I empty out, I will run back to you to fill back up. Thank you for every miracle. Thank you for faith that changes me and the world around me.

3

We Will Live in Truth

A Spirit-Led Heart Is Defined by Truth

God's Spirit challenges us to hear truth, admit truth, and receive truth.

Jennifer Rothschild, *Me, Myself, and Lies*

She and her siblings clung to each other, hoping that one day it would get better. She married a man when she was too young, because that's what you do when it is the best escape plan. Her husband made a promise to love and cherish her. He promptly forgot that promise once the ring was slipped on her finger. She loves Jesus. She's a warrior when it comes to her children. She's fought for everything she's ever had.

Despite her struggles, she's one of the strongest people I know. One day we were hanging out, and our conversation led to the topic of love. It's a confusing topic to her, because love hasn't been lived very well in front of her.

We read Romans 8 together, and the words pierced. Tears brimmed as my friend read portions out loud more than once. The Holy Spirit was doing something for my friend that I couldn't.

"I get it now," she said. "I'm worth loving because God chose to love me first."

My friend had received a thousand messages that she was un-lovable. That memo was deeply ingrained in her mind. There was a closed-off space in her that didn't dare believe she was worthy of love.

Have you ever had a moment when truth is suddenly clear?

It's been obscure, murky. You've tried to figure it out on your own, perhaps for years. It feels as though everybody else "gets it" except for you. That's how my friend felt until the message in Romans 8 leaped from the pages and settled into her spiritual DNA.

> For I am convinced that neither death nor life, neither angels nor demons, neither the present nor the future, nor any powers, neither height nor depth, nor anything else in all creation, will be able to separate us from the love of God that is in Christ Jesus our Lord.
>
> Romans 8:38–39

Truth overpowered a lie she believed for far too long.

No one has ever loved me well, so I must be unlovable.

That lie felt like truth, which hindered her in different ways, from self-esteem to self-preservation. It made her a survivor. She felt that she had to be on the defensive emotionally. It made her skeptical. If someone showed her love, they must have an ulterior motive. They wanted something from her, and if she gave in, the walls would come tumbling down.

As she read Romans 8, she laughed richly. I wanted to harvest that joy, it was so tangible. She laughed because she was God's daughter. This truth, inspired by the Holy Spirit, was setting her free. She is a child of God and is loved like crazy. For the first time, she felt qualified to call out "Abba, Father."

It was more than words. It was truth.

Counselors might call this a breakthrough. It's that moment when you see yourself or a situation differently, and suddenly you reframe a past event to include hope for today. You are liberated from negative words spoken over you or expectations or limitations that have nothing to do with God's plan for you.

Truth is a spiritual weapon (Ephesians 6:14).

It's one of the arsenal in the battle against an enemy whose goal is to mire God's daughters in toothless lies. Truth penetrates. It divides and separates. It exposes false teaching that has a hint of truth but leads away from God rather than toward him. It sorts through manipulation and clouded messages so that we can see clearly.

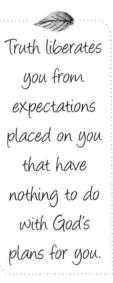

Truth liberates you from expectations placed on you that have nothing to do with God's plans for you.

Lies had shaped my friend's view of herself and of her worth. Some of those lies led her in a direction God never intended for her. Like insecurity. Like shooting down dreams, because she didn't believe she deserved to dream. Some of those lies kept her from receiving good things. She had heard this Scripture in Romans 8 numerous times, but this time it was different.

This time the words were for *her*.

Truth liberated her from others' sins that entangled her innocent heart (Romans 8:2). Long ago she had been set free from her own sin. Now she was being set free from the effects of an abusive father and a neglectful spouse. She was being set free from lies that felt like truth. As we sat on the steps together, with tears running down her face, she marveled that this truth had been there all along, just waiting for her to discover.

That led her to another question.

What other truths were waiting to set her free?

The Early Church: Does Truth Matter?

Little white lies. Gray areas. Half-truths.

These phrases are common. They take truth and provide margins around it. They give us room to slip and slide when truth feels uncomfortable. They allow lies to infiltrate and set themselves up as fact. Truth isn't always comfortable. I may not want to speak it. I may not want to hear it. If it's God's truth and it asks me to forgive, to sacrifice something I love, to be honest about my vulnerabilities, or to turn the other cheek, I may substitute truth for something that feels a little less painful.

This is one struggle in the quest for truth.

The other is that it's hard to know what is true. The amount of data we take in every day is staggering. It's hard to unplug, and some of us never do. We take in more data in a day than our great-great-grandparents absorbed in a lifetime. We are told what to believe, what to do, what to wear, what to buy, and what to think. We are hyperconnected, overly entertained, and involved in people's lives in ways that didn't exist a handful of years ago. "Truth" is shared, tweeted, retweeted, posted, and tagged even when it has no basis in truth at all.

Then there is our personal struggle with truth.

We've heard words used to describe us or tell us who we are. Those words may have been shared by someone out of pain, addiction, rage, or a lack of insight or maturity, yet we believe them. We live as if they are gospel.

We also sort through truth about our faith. This is shaped by doctrine, by people who live their faith in close proximity, and through the examples of others in the public eye, on social media, in traditional media, and in church. We may grow up thinking that God is continually angry at us. Or we may intentionally sin because we believe grace offers a free pass. We may not know what to believe.

Truth *matters.*

That's painfully evident in Acts 5:1–10. The early church is building a strong community. They pool resources, including food, coins, land, and property. Those combined resources take care of the basic needs of the growing church. It is also used for those among them who can't care for themselves, such as the poor and hungry.

It's a powerful image of a church at work.

Ananias and his wife, Sapphira, are a part of that close-knit community. One day they sell their land and take the funds to the apostle Peter.

> Now a man named Ananias, together with his wife Sapphira, also sold a piece of property. With his wife's full knowledge he kept back part of the money for himself, but brought the rest and put it at the apostles' feet. Then Peter said, "Ananias, how is it that Satan has so filled your heart that you have lied to the Holy Spirit and have kept for yourself some of the money you received for the land? Didn't it belong to you before it was sold? And after it was sold, wasn't the money at your disposal? What made you think of doing such a thing? You have not lied just to human beings but to God."
>
> Acts 5:1–4

Why lie? No one is forced to donate or sell their property. No one is coerced to give. It is their money to do with however they desire. Perhaps they have hidden the real amount so that others will applaud their generosity. Perhaps on their way to see Peter they had a fight about how much to give.

We aren't certain. All we know is that Ananias makes a show of giving all the money from the sale while secretly holding a portion back, and that his wife is in on the deceit.

No one is fooled. The Holy Spirit reveals the truth to Peter. When the money is placed in his hands, he already knows what is true and what is false. He also knows there is a consequence to Ananias's lie.

Ananias drops to the ground dead. Tragically, Sapphira also dies.

When I first read this years ago, I thought their punishment was harsh.

Should they have been called out for lying? Sure. Did they deserve death? I struggled with that. I don't applaud lying, but they gave part of the money. That seems generous, right? They didn't have to give any of it. This is where my westernized thinking slipped in.

A little white lie. A gray area. A half-truth.

Many believe that truth is an option. Peter tells Ananias that he lied not only to him, but to God. Truth matters to God. We shouldn't worry that a lie will cause us to drop dead, but it's wise to value truth and integrity. We are in a battle with an enemy who is the ultimate truth twister (John 8:44; 2 Corinthians 11:14). Shading the truth might feel harmless—unless you are the one trying to figure out what the truth is.

Ananias and Sapphira's lie is jarring.

The apostles are the face of the early church. They walked with Jesus, and that makes them targets. Their presence stirs curious crowds. The sick are prayed over, and many are healed. The apostles are jailed and severely beaten frequently. They live under constant scrutiny. Every word, every sermon, every action is judged. They refuse to hide because they have too much to do.

Time is of the essence. They have only one life to give. They won't waste a minute.

This community is a safe place for the apostles and for the church. Sapphira and Ananias are friends. When they lie to Peter, they make it harder to know whom to trust, and that is weighty.

You didn't just lie to me, you lied to God.

Peter saw the consequence coming before Ananias did.

Their lies could expose the church to criticism. It might cause a person on the edge of following Jesus to turn the other way. Their lies have the power to discourage those who are giving everything. It weaves deceit into a community supposed to reflect Jesus.

There are times when I want to skip past a passage in the Bible, and this is one of them.

Plenty of people lie or cheat or skirt integrity to get what they want, and we don't see them falling like flies on the pavement.

God isn't poised to strike us when we make a mistake. However, he is a God of truth. He is a protector. He reacted quickly to a lie that had the ability to discourage those fighting in the trenches. It's a rarity with God, this type of punishment, but Sapphira and Ananias didn't just lie to Peter. They lied to God. Their lies might be instruments of division and discouragement in a holy work.

This gives me pause.

I love that God allows me to partner in ministry with him. I'm not afraid of being struck down by my heavenly Father, but I want to respect the fact that he requires integrity whether anyone is watching or not. Whether it benefits me or not. Lies may come back to haunt me, but what's more important, they have the power to trip up others on their way to Jesus. If it comes down to telling a painful truth or a half-truth/gray area/little white lie, choosing truth delights the heart of God.

Truth matters.

It's our spiritual defense. It's light in a dark room. It is life. It illuminates our understanding of the Word; it lights our path (Psalm 119:105). Truth changes us. It redirects us when we are going the opposite of God's best.

Lies? They tangle us up. They destroy reputations and dreams. They cause us to mistrust people—and sometimes God—because people have hurt us.

Truth matters.

Have I already mentioned that? It's why it is so important to know the difference between what is true and what is not.

Your Promise: The Holy Spirit Leads into Truth

In my book *The Unburdened Heart*, I share the story of a phone call with my biological father. Though I hadn't spoken to him but a few times in my entire life, he was losing a battle with cancer. I called because I wanted him to know that I cared. Shortly after he answered, the call took a downward turn.

He told me that he didn't want my prayers or my concern. As he ended the conversation, he said, "I'm not even sure you are mine."

This was an opportunity for lies to explode in a woman's heart. My intention in making the call was pure. The result was a mess, as a lie tried to creep in and take root.

You must be pretty unlovable if your biological father denies you on his deathbed.

I sat with my phone in my hand.

I was a mom to three young adults and couldn't imagine saying those words to them. I couldn't imagine not being in their lives. Like a zip line without brakes, my thoughts started to fly. Jennifer Rothschild, author of *Me, Myself, and Lies* describes this as self-talk.

> The words we say go straight to the core of our being. They shape the way we think about ourselves. They influence our emotions and our decisions. They resurface in our conversations with other people. They can spur us on to live meaningful, productive lives, or they can make us not even want to get out of bed![1]

My thoughts carried just as much weight as they would if I were shouting from the rooftop.

It was important that truth find its rightful place in this scenario. Was I sad? I was.

Did it hurt? It did.

Did it make me feel foolish for calling? A little bit.

Was the accuser in my ear whispering that I was unloved and unwanted? Absolutely.

Yet my feelings weren't the complete truth. I am incredibly loved by a lot of people. I am loved by my heavenly Father. I don't know why my biological father said the words that he did. He was terminally ill and suffering. I don't know whether he meant them or was lashing out and I just happened to be in the way.

This is what I do know, because it's grounded in scriptural truth.

His words cut, but I didn't have to embrace them or nurture them. They did not have to become my identity. The Lord was with me in that moment, and he cared for us both. I could sit there and nurture those confused emotions, or run toward truth.

Just because you believe a lie doesn't make it true. That's important to consider in moments like these.

Is it a truth or a lie?

That's the question we are compelled to ask, and the Holy Spirit will bring the answer to light. If it's based on the words of a broken person, it's most likely a distortion of the truth. If it's wrapped up in emotions, we might not be able to see the truth yet.

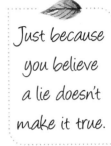

Just because you believe a lie doesn't make it true.

We need to turn away from that person, that circumstance, that feeling, and ask that truth be spoken by the Holy Spirit. Our Helper helps us remember truth, for he is truth (1 John 5:6). He can't and won't lead us in the wrong direction.

> For you created my inmost being; you knit me together in my mother's womb. I praise you because I am fearfully and wonderfully made; your works are wonderful, I know that full well. My frame was not hidden from you when I was made in the secret place, when I was woven together in the depths of the earth. Your eyes saw my unformed body; all the days ordained for me were written in your book before one of them came to be.
>
> Psalm 139:13–16

That was my truth. It continues to be my truth. God knows me well. Every hair, every quirk, every gifting. I am loved by him. I have a purpose. I don't have to show off, prove anything, or measure up to earn that love. Knowing the truth isn't just about feelings or emotions. The Holy Spirit activates our faith. That's his role. When we know the truth, we live the truth.

My biological father died shortly after that conversation. I drove to the funeral in another state and stood at the casket of a man I barely knew. I spent time with his other children in his home. They were kind and open. We looked at old photo albums, and they shared memories of him. They showed me pictures of my sister and me when we were tiny. He had placed the pictures carefully in an album. As I drove home, tears fell. This time they were tears of gratitude. His son told me that on his father's deathbed, a kind man led our biological father to Christ. In his last hours, he found the peace that had evaded him most of his life.

When we know the truth, we live the truth.

Truth allowed me to take the focus off myself and celebrate his homecoming.

When lies feel like truth, we have a choice to make. We can allow those messages to define us, or we can live by truth. A dying man's words were not the complete story. His words had less to do with me than they did with his brokenness. The Holy Spirit freed me from the impact of his words, but also led to compassion for him. I hadn't walked in his shoes. I didn't know his story. I don't know how lies influenced him as a child and into adulthood.

Furthermore, I was not obligated to spend the rest of my life trying to figure it all out. I could rejoice that he had found Jesus, even if it was in his last hours.

When we welcome attributes of the Holy Spirit, we affirm God himself.

We accept his word as true. We seek his thoughts over our own. Our inner core is strengthened even as our outer bodies and heart are battered.

Freedom! That's where truth leads us.

When we don't know who is telling the truth or whether a person's motivation is pure, the temptation is to be cynical. When a lie damages our sense of self, the temptation is to build walls that keep everybody out, even the good ones. When we are tempted to allow a lie to take root, we may believe that the only person we can trust is ourselves, and that's lonely. When we believe lies that say we are unworthy, we miss out on the greatest love story of all time.

Lies hold us captive. They are an accusation from the enemy. They hammer at the identity and purpose of a daughter of God, and that's unacceptable.

Truth unravels those lies and sets us free.

Your Invitation: Choose Truth, Choose Life

When my friend and I sat with the Bible open to Romans 8, it was like watching a flower open on a spring day. Sin had taunted my friend. Sinful choices made by others led her to think in a way that robbed her.

> Therefore, brothers and sisters, we have an obligation—but it is not to the flesh, to live according to it. For if you live according to the flesh, you will die; *but if by the Spirit* you put to death the misdeeds of the body, you will live.
>
> Romans 8:12–13

I love *The Message* translation of this Scripture:

> So don't you see that we don't owe this old do-it-yourself life one red cent. There's nothing in it for us, nothing at all. The best thing to do is give it a decent burial and get on with your new life. *God's Spirit beckons.* There are things to do and places to go!

Romans 8 reminds us that the Holy Spirit puts sin to death, but it doesn't stop there. When sin is put to death, we are given new life! Paul is referring to freedom from our own sin, but this is just as powerful when we apply it to sin wounds left by others. We aren't obligated to (responsible for or in agreement with) sin's power over us, because it was put to death on the cross once and for all.

So what can we do?

Choose truth over lies every time.

Lies lead to assumptions, which become beliefs, which produce actions (or inactions) that impact your life and your identity.

Let's look at how that might play out in our own hearts.

Lie	Assumption/Belief	Actions
You can never change.	It's just who I am.	• Feeling trapped • Not taking risks, even healthy ones • Giving up easily • Comparison • Frustration
That's your lot in life.	It's what we do. (It's what people like me do.)	• Identifying with the past, people, dysfunction, or labels placed on you rather than with your identity as a child of God
You're so [fill in the blank].	It's what is expected of me.	• Allowing other people to define how smart, talented, gifted, valuable, worthy, or loved you are • Receiving negative words as truth • Resisting when someone tries to tell you otherwise • Having a tarnished view of people and situations
You've messed up too badly.	It's all I deserve.	• People pleasing • Trying harder • Perfection • Continually trying to prove to yourself and others that you are good

When we think of death, we usually think of physical death. But a lack of truth leads to spiritual death. We accept the opposite of what we are promised by God. We live as if we are not daughters and heirs. But our Savior didn't come so that we may have death—he came so that we may have life that is abundant and full (John 10:10).

We are not obligated to sin.

We aren't responsible to live another person's lie as if it were true. We don't have to be in agreement with it. We aren't beholden to it. It's not ours to carry for years and years, or to pass down to the next generation.

As my friend examined the lies she had received and the damage they left behind, it freed her to look at a different road. She was not obligated to sin, but free to do something different. She was free to be who she really was rather than what someone said she was. She was free to carve a new path, not just for herself, but for those who come after her. She is free to go in the reverse direction of negative expectations.

Maybe lies have led you down a road that you hate. Exchange those lies for truth.

The lie that feels like truth	The truth that sets you free
The lie: It's just who I am.	*Truth:* I am free to be who God made me to be.
The lie: It's what we (my family, my culture, my people) do.	*Truth:* I am free to carve a new path, even if generations before me went a different way.
The lie: It's what is expected of me.	*Truth:* I am free to go the opposite direction of anyone's expectations except for God's.
↓	↓
Obligation leads to death—spiritual, emotional, physical.	Truth leads to life—spiritual, emotional, physical, eternal.

When Jesus walked with the disciples, he poured truth over them. He challenged them, asking them to put what they learned into practice.

> *But when he, the Spirit of truth, comes, he will guide you into all the truth.* He will not speak on his own; he will speak only what he hears, and he will tell you what is yet to come.
>
> John 16:13

We put truth into practice as we study truth. We aren't afraid to ask questions, even the hard ones. The longer we live and practice truth, the more natural it becomes to follow the truth.

The Holy Spirit is our Helper in every part of it.

- He teaches us (1 John 2:27).
- He brings truth to remembrance when we need it most (John 14:26).
- He shows us what is real and what is false (1 John 4:6).

Truth becomes a safe place (Proverbs 2:11) as we feed and nurture our souls with the help of the Holy Spirit.

Truth without Borders

As we fill up with truth, there is less room for lies. When we fill up with the Word, what is true, what is lovely, what is pure, what is uplifting, and what is praiseworthy (Philippians 4:8) make themselves at home. There will always be a battle: half-truths, gray areas, and little white lies versus honesty and integrity. That's our culture. That's the all-out war waged by an enemy who desires to distract you from God's love for you. But when truth becomes your go-to, it becomes your spiritual weapon.

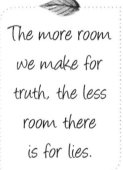

The more room we make for truth, the less room there is for lies.

The Holy Spirit uses truth to fight for you. You seek it. You choose it. You live by it. You hold truth in high regard.

Truth is rare in a culture where half-truths, gray areas, and lies thrive, but if it leads to life and freedom, others can't help but notice the difference.

A person who walks in truth lives without the constraints of lies. They are free to be who God knows they can be. They are free to follow Jesus, even if a thousand people try to convince them otherwise. They are free to admit that they are flawed and apologize when they mess up.

What truth does the Holy Spirit long to reveal to you?

What lie is he asking you to put down?

My friend is still on a journey toward truth. She's thrown away those heavy weights like unwanted trash. Maybe it will take a lifetime, but every time she discovers a new truth, she is hungry to discover the next.

Ask the Helper to show you truth. Ask him to help you recognize it. Toss out that lie you've embraced as truth for far too long, for when you know the truth, you are free to live the truth.

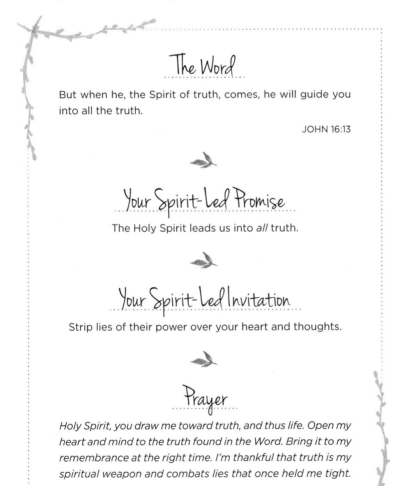

The Word

But when he, the Spirit of truth, comes, he will guide you into all the truth.

JOHN 16:13

Your Spirit-Led Promise

The Holy Spirit leads us into *all* truth.

Your Spirit-Led Invitation

Strip lies of their power over your heart and thoughts.

Prayer

Holy Spirit, you draw me toward truth, and thus life. Open my heart and mind to the truth found in the Word. Bring it to my remembrance at the right time. I'm thankful that truth is my spiritual weapon and combats lies that once held me tight.

4

We Will Never Wander

A Spirit-Led Heart Finds Direction

Trying to do the Lord's work in your own strength is the most confusing, exhausting, and tedious of all work. But when you are filled with the Holy Spirit, then the ministry of Jesus just flows out of you.

Corrie ten Boom

I was thrilled at the invitation to go to India. I would be part of the International Initiatives team representing Proverbs 31 Ministries. They were partnering with Mission India, a literacy program that reached thousands of girls and women who didn't have access to education. The trip was planned for the next year.

The first hint that things were about to change came in a text from my friend Amy, the team leader.

"Suz, the trip is pulling together much quicker than we thought it would. Are you available this year instead of next?"

I looked at my digital calendar. Red, blue, and green stripes stared back at me. I flipped to September and October, which were somewhat empty. July and August were crowded.

March, April, and May were crammed. I was launching a book, *Come with Me*. I was in the middle of writing a new devotional book, and the deadline was early May. I was planning a retreat. Fifty women were flying in from around the country in mid-April, and there were a thousand details to finish. I ~~prayed~~ bargained with God.

I'd love to do this, as long as it's not the last three weeks of April or the first week of May.

Then I laughed at my silliness.

There was no way that a trip could be organized that quickly for seven people, traveling from different parts of the United States, to visit north, central, and southern India.

I sent my response. I'd love to go.

If it fits in my calendar. In my timing. As long as it's convenient for me.

No, I didn't say any of those, but it's what I meant.

The second message arrived a few days later. "We've picked out dates. The trip will be somewhere in the last three weeks of April or the first week of May. Get your shots. Start taking your malaria meds. Make sure your passport is up to date. The trip is on!"

I sat with my head in my hands. I wanted to go. I thought I was supposed to go, but it wasn't possible. I held up my laptop, as if God didn't know every detail of my life. I showed Jesus the red and blue and green stripes on my calendar one more time, as if to prove my point.

My reply to the team leader was going to sound polite and very spiritual: *Unfortunately, the timing won't work. I'm so excited that this opens the door for someone else to go. I'll be praying for the team! Wish I could be with you.*

As I sat with my cell phone in my hands, grief was in the details.

God knows my heart. There's nothing more I desire than to watch faith tangibly impact women. I have books on my shelves marked and underlined. There are books stacked in nooks and corners that describe the plight of women. My journal is filled with prayers for women I have never met.

When I was first asked to be a part of the International Initiatives team, I wept. It was a dream come true. While others might not see holding a child with lice-infested hair, eating unfamiliar food, or ministering in dusty streets or rag-picking slums as a gift, it is to me.

Poised to send my answer of no, I paused.

There are those moments when the inner voice of the Holy Spirit is confirming or comforting, but sometimes it's convicting. I realized that I had more concern over launching a book about following Jesus than I had for actually following him. I glanced one more time at my calendar. You know, the one stacked with ministry deadlines and to-dos—the ministry that's about Jesus. I wasn't sure how I was going to do it, but I was supposed to go.

While not every assignment is mine, this one was.

I typed my answer.

I'm in.

The Early Church: Drifting versus Directed

Despite the apostles' peaceful ways, the Sanhedrin plot to harm them and their cause. The church is rapidly growing, and the religious authorities are uneasy about how many have been added to their number.

Three thousand here. Five thousand there.

They've tried jailing them. They've tried beating them. The pesky apostles and Jesus followers just go right back to preaching and teaching. The authorities gather for a plotting session. They want to figure out how to silence these Jesus followers once and for all.

A prominent Pharisee named Gamaliel steps up to reason with them. He reminds them of a guy named Theudas who claimed to be somebody important. When he died, all his followers went away. He tells the story of Judas the Galilean, who led a revolt in the city. Similar to Theudas, once he died, his followers went back to their ordinary lives.

Gamaliel shared this advice:

"Therefore, in the present case I advise you: Leave these men alone! Let them go! For if their purpose or activity is of human origin, it will fail. But if it is from God, you will not be able to stop these men; you will only find yourselves fighting against God."

Acts 5:38–39

If the Sanhedrin follow Gamaliel's advice, they will avoid negative backlash from the community. They will let these followers exhaust themselves, and the church will fade away.

Whether they know it or not, Gamaliel's words are prophetic. *If God is in it, you can't stop it.*

Jesus told the disciples they'd be "witnesses in Jerusalem, and in all Judea and Samaria, and to the ends of the earth" (Acts 1:8). They don't know that the gospel will reach thousands of years into the future. The promise, however, is that if God is in the details, man can't destroy their work.

The leaders call the apostles in and have them beaten one more time for good measure. Once again, they warn them to shut their mouths about this man called Jesus.

If God is in it, man can't destroy it.

The apostles leave, their backs bruised and bleeding. But their hands are in the air as they rejoice at the privilege of suffering disgrace in the name of Jesus.

Every day they go to the temple and preach. They travel from house to house to share the news that Jesus is the Messiah. Persecution is curbed for a season, but it heats back up because the apostles never stop doing what Jesus asked them to do.

From the outside looking in, it seems that the early church is doomed. They don't have a lot of resources. They don't have a building or a master blueprint. They only have the words of the Master.

Go.

If God is in it, then a lack of resources, harsh conditions, or harsh people can't stop it. The very things that should destroy them will eventually be the catalyst for spreading the gospel. Peter will land in Rome, under the persecution of Nero. Andrew will travel to modern-day Georgia, Asia Minor, and modern-day Turkey, and be martyred in Greece. Thomas will land in Syria, and Philip in North Africa. Judas (not Iscariot) will minister in Mesopotamia, and Matthew will serve in Ethiopia and Persia. Bartholomew will travel widely—to India, Armenia, Ethiopia, and eventually South Arabia. James (the son of Alpheus) and Matthias (who replaced Judas Iscariot) will locate in Syria. Simon the Zealot ends up in Persia. John leads a church in Ephesus.

They don't know any of this. All they have are Jesus's words to *go*.

They aren't without direction, however. They preach the word wherever they are (Acts 8:4). They plant the gospel in every circumstance. If they are around a dinner table, they share their message with friends. If they are in jail, they look for someone who doesn't know the gospel. Their direction isn't a place, but the privilege of spreading the gospel. Around the table. Face to face. In sweet times of community. And smack in the heart of adversity.

All the while they are being launched into worldwide ministry. An apostle here. An apostle there. A church here. A church there. A word in good times. A word when it is hard. The breath of the Holy Spirit in one place, wonders and miracles in another. They don't see the bigger picture, but it is being painted stroke by stroke, and they are part of the masterpiece.

They experience anxious moments. They toil long hours. They walk long days. They cross rough seas. They pray for unbelievers. They start churches from scratch. They discover that people are both wonderful and a pain. They experience fatigue and overwhelming joy. Yet they are home wherever they land, whatever situation they are in.

Going means being authentic to their faith wherever they are.

We may define direction as a place or a timeline, but the early church defined it as being directed by the Holy Spirit no matter where they were.

Maybe you've asked the following questions. I have.
Where is God leading?
What is my purpose?
Do I wait? Do I stay here? Do I make a bold move?
Why is this so hard?

These are questions we all have asked. We won't always be in the know. It's nice when that happens, but if God is in it (in you, in the heart of your plans, in that dream he placed within you, as you listen for his voice daily), then nothing can stop his plans for you.

> Direction isn't about where we are; it's who is on God's heart as we go.

They may look different from how you think they should. The timing may not line up with yours. But direction isn't about where we are; it's about who is on God's heart as we go.

> "But you will *receive power when the Holy Spirit comes upon you.* And you will be my witnesses, telling people about me everywhere—in Jerusalem, throughout Judea, in Samaria, and to the ends of the earth."
>
> Acts 1:8 NLT

These words transition us from building a church to becoming the church.

We will never wander. We are at home in that new church community. We are at home in that in-between job. We are at home in the waiting seasons.

Your Promise: You Will Never Be Lost

Maybe you've struggled with direction because you've been waiting for God to lay a location on your heart. You'd love for God to spell it out for you.

Step one—Go here. Do this.

Step two—Take a hard right.

Step three—I'll provide in this manner.

Step four—Go here.

It rarely works that way.

When we measure spiritual direction the same way we measure things in our natural lives, we fail to take in the faith factor. If God is in the plan, it won't be stopped. That gives us permission to stop rushing it. To rest in his time frame. Challenges don't make us want to give up. We surrender to his plans right where we are.

We no longer equate *go* with *do*, for the Lord equated *go* with *be*.

Be a witness wherever you are, whether on a fast track or in training. Be ready whether rocking a child in your arms or rocking in an airplane on the way to a mission field.

Be open, even in a waiting time.

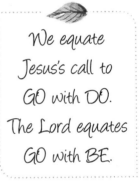

We equate Jesus's call to GO with DO. The Lord equates GO with BE.

This past summer I felt the Lord asking me to slow down. I had been in a season of intense writing and traveling. Richard's and my parents were aging and needed us. I felt the Holy Spirit directing me to slow things down a bit. Just for a few months.

Can I be frank with you?

Slowing down felt like failure. I equated going with doing instead of with being.

I summed it up like this: Less activity = less direction.

I feared that if I wasn't doing something all the time, ministry would fade away. As if it depended on me.

Oh, Father, help me. Forgive me for believing that I'm somehow responsible for carrying the weight of this ministry or your calling on my life. Isn't it crazy that I somehow think that, if I obey you, things will fall apart without me? This was never about me or my efforts. In your mercy, adjust my heart (and my thinking) one more time.

Just sharing that makes me feel vulnerable, but it was my prayer. I wrote it in my journal. God leads us daily. We can plan, and we will, but if he's in it (the waiting times, the go times), we are exactly where we should be.

Listen to Galamiel's words one more time.

> "If they are planning and doing these things merely on their own, it will soon be overthrown. But if it is from God, you will not be able to overthrow them. You may even find yourselves fighting against God!"
>
> Acts 5:38–39 NLT

If God is in this waiting phase of your life, then it's not going to fall apart if you release it to him. If it does, then it probably needed to be put down. If the Holy Spirit is leading you to release something or step into a season of waiting or refueling, listen to him.

I gave myself permission to fill back up after writing 400,000-plus words in the last two years. If I hadn't, I would have burned out, bummed out, or kept running on fumes. I don't want to be that woman pretending that I can tell you how to live free if I'm in bondage myself.

My answer to the Lord was joyful surrender. I slowed down. I worked, but at a gentler pace for a short season. I was still doing. I was going.

Primarily I was *being.*

Being sensitive to his leading. Being at rest spiritually. Finding a rhythm that matched God's plan for me rather than what I thought ministry or life should look like.

As disciples of Christ, we will have plans and goals—whether for ministry, careers, lives, or families. We are wise to pray for direction and wisdom. A Spirit-led heart reframes the usual questions to find the God factor. When we do this, we find direction.

What we might ask	Asking for Spirit-led direction
What is my purpose?	What is on your heart, God?
Why is this taking so long?	What are you trying to teach me?
Why did you lead me here?	What part do you want me to play, right where I am?

Reframing the questions repositions our hearts.

Isn't that part of seeking direction? We trust that God has a purpose for us, and we seek his heart in the matter. We believe that he planted that dream, but we don't wait for a final destination to be effective and fruitful. If we are in a place where we don't want to be, but we've prayed and followed him, we start to look for the ministry or training in this part of the journey.

Every part of our lives counts. If God is in it, there's something taking place that we might not understand until eternity. That redefines our view of success, especially when we look at the early church.

How do we listen for the voice of the Holy Spirit?

It's a nudge. It's an urgency that won't go away. It's Scripture leaping from the pages and showing us something we didn't see the time before. It's a godly man or woman praying with us or over us, and prophetic words landing in that tender spot in our soul, and we know it's God. His voice will never contradict Scripture, for the Holy Spirit always leads us closer to God and his will.

You may be uncertain about where you'll land when the dust clears, but there's peace in the process.

Peace is there whether it's easy or not. You may have questions, but there's an inner knowing that you are headed in the right direction—even if that's standing still for a season. You listen for details but aren't afraid to allow him to rearrange those details. As you listen for the voice of the Holy Spirit, it becomes familiar.

There are many examples of the early church listening to the Holy Spirit.

The two of them, *sent on their way by the Holy Spirit*, went down to Seleucia and sailed from there to Cyprus.

Acts 13:4

> *Where we go isn't nearly as important as having a heart ready to go.*

The Spirit told Philip, "Go to that chariot and stay near it."

Acts 8:29

The apostles didn't define direction with words like *open doors* or *smooth sailing*. The rough spots (lingering, difficult circumstances, naysayers) were often where walking with Jesus made the greatest impact. If they felt the Holy Spirit leading, they turned around. They climbed into that chariot. Where they went wasn't nearly as important as having a heart ready to go, whatever that looked like.

Your Invitation: Accept Your Assignment

My car has 170,000 miles on the odometer. Richard's has over 225,000. We hop in a car and think nothing of it. It's not unusual for me to drive a four- to six-hour round trip on a Saturday to attend the birthday party of a loved one. We make trips to see our parents, who all live across state lines. Mileage is just a number.

Not so for the early church.

They traveled mostly by foot and often walked up to a rugged pace of twenty miles a day. It wasn't unusual for entire families to spend their lifetime within a fifty-mile radius. A traveler needed to know where to find springs of water or wells along the way. The terrain was rough and often dangerous. They were exposed to robbers and bandits as well as the elements and wild animals. Traveling by boat or ship was just as treacherous due to tumultuous storms and rough waters.

We don't have these same challenges, so why does it feel so treacherous for us?

The fear is in the details.

Lord, did you really just ask me to talk to my neighbor as she waters her garden?

Lord, this is stretching me so much.

You want me to do what?

You know that isn't my strength!

Remember my red-, blue-, and green-striped calendar? It's how I roll. It's how God made me. If I don't have a schedule, I'm going to miss something.

There's nothing wrong with having a plan, unless the plan becomes greater than the assignment.

Our invitation is to accept that assignment and discover what God is trying to teach us.

Spirit-Led Direction without Borders

Four weeks after my text from my friend Amy, I boarded a plane for New York, then continued on to India. All my major April events were behind me. I leaned back in my seat, thinking about the past few weeks. They had rushed by. Fifty women arrived at the retreat and it had been amazing. I met my book deadline.

There was still a lot to do. My book *Come with Me* would release two days after I returned from India. I had another speaking engagement just after that.

We slept all night on the plane and finally arrived in Delhi. The temperature was 111 degrees when we stepped outside the airport. For the next several days we visited church plants, literacy programs, and mission headquarters in several regions of India. We traveled on twelve planes in ten days. We brainstormed, prayed, and worshiped. We rode in cars late at night and got back in them early the following morning for the next destination.

Traffic in India is like a giant snarling game of chicken. I often held a useless seat belt across my chest as I rode in the back seat, sometimes with my eyes closed, other times fascinated by a family of five on a scooter built for two whizzing by my window. Dad drove in front, with two small children squeezed between him and Mom as she sat sidesaddle, an infant tucked in her arms.

As the days passed, I was thrilled to be there but uncertain of my assignment.

I was waiting to check something off my list. You know, something that said, *This is why I wanted you to go, Suzie.* One day we drove to a rag-picking slum. A little girl, no more than eighteen months old, wore a ragged white dress and no diaper or underpants. I knelt in front of her and noticed a jagged cut on her ankle. It was from the low-hanging barbed wire she had just climbed through. I dug through my backpack, looking for a bandage.

My Gaga heart hurt for her. There wasn't a bandage big enough to fix what was wrong with this picture. I've traveled to many nations. I love cross-cultural ministry. I've witnessed poverty, yet this was different. We encountered darkness and oppression, especially against women and little girls. This little girl was Dalit, an "untouchable" class even lower than the lowest recognized caste. I had met her mother and grandmother, who were in the literacy program.

It takes a lot to overwhelm me, but as I knelt in front of that beautiful child, I was overwhelmed. I was overwhelmed by what I couldn't come close to fixing. I was overwhelmed by the women I talked to who were persecuted for following Jesus. I was overwhelmed by the scars that women privately revealed to me—scars from husbands or mothers-in-law beating them.

India is beautiful, and there are many strong and good men and women. There are people fighting for justice. There are those who buck persecution (just like the disciples) to do what is right for their people. India is a democratic secular nation where religion is supposed to be accessible, yet I listened to stories of subtle and overt harassment—from landlords taking away the rights to live in a humble home to government officials threatening the loss of a job.

I was overwhelmed, even with the good. I reluctantly sat in a place of honor in a too-warm metal shack as women and girls read an elementary primer with pride—women and girls who were refused dignity because of a lack of birthright. I sampled homemade toothpaste and pain rub, rejoicing with women who learned how to make these items and start small businesses on the street.

I looked for Jesus in the slum. I needed to see him there. Tears fell often.

I listened to stories of Jesus healing a child, or the first moment a woman realized there was one God. I hugged my Christian sister who discovered that she didn't have to earn or beg for the favor of a plethora of gods or be stuck in an eternal game of karma.

Yet out of the twenty-plus international trips I've made over the last twenty years, this one left me struggling to know why I was there.

I couldn't get away from that moment when I held my laptop up to Jesus, showing him my busy life and feeling that overwhelming nudge that this was my assignment.

I was struggling with that same old war of *doing* versus *being*.

One night, five of us traveled to a late-night literacy class. We prayed with the women, and it was late when we left. Back in the car, the lead ministry partner turned to face my friend Lynn and me in the back seat. "I know it's late," he said, "but a friend of mine's wife is sick. She's on her way home from the hospital after a chemotherapy treatment. Would you mind if we dropped by and prayed for her?"

He was hesitant.

It was after nine in the evening, and the traffic was still unbelievably difficult. His friend and wife lived in the opposite direction of our lodging. At best, we'd arrive home around midnight. At worst, it could be much later. "I told her that we were partnering with a women's ministry this week," he said, "and that one of the women was a cancer survivor. She's excited that we are coming."

Lynn and I both said, "Let's go!"

When we arrived at the apartment, Lynn sat on the couch nearby. I sat next to the woman. A mint green scarf covered what was left of her hair. Tiredness marked her eyes and posture. It was after nine, but she had just returned from the hospital after a chemo treatment. We talked for a few moments, sharing common stories of battling cancer. I started to tell her a little bit about what God did during my battle with cancer years earlier. The whole time she stared at me intently. She put her hand on my cheek, an uncommon gesture for an Indian woman.

"You are Suzie Eller," she said quietly.

It had been a 110-plus-degree day. We'd started that morning early, with little sleep the night before. Lynn's hair was in a ponytail. I had clipped part of mine off my face. We were red-faced, and our clothing clung to us. We barely recognized ourselves. We hadn't made introductions, not yet.

"How do you know that?" I asked.

She recognized me (and Lynn) because she had been meeting with us every morning for years. I've been part of a beautiful ministry called Proverbs 31 Ministries for over a decade. For most of those years, I've served as a volunteer writer for a daily devotion called *Encouragement for Today*. It's a free devotion that goes out to more than a million women across the world.

On each devotion, there's a tiny picture of the writer. This woman was one of the over one million women who receive this devotion. While I sat there stunned, she told us how that small piece of email encouraged her each day. It made her feel as though she was sitting with other faith-filled women. She told me details about my life. Details I had written in devotions over the years. "I remember that story about your grandson," she said, smiling. "The one with the yellow floaties."

Then she said, "I often prayed that one day I could travel to the U.S. to thank all of you for these encouragements, but God in his mercy brought you to my front door in my lowest hour."

We remained with her for several more minutes. We laughed. We prayed.

When Lynn and I climbed in the car, we looked at each other *Did that really just happen?*

Our earthly plans will never measure up to God's heavenly assignments.

This woman didn't know we were coming. We were on the other side of the city, with plans to fly out in the morning. She had prayed to meet us one day.

India has 1.2 billion people. It has the largest number of unreached people groups in the world as far as Christianity is concerned. You won't find people having casual conversations about Christianity in the street, because you don't live as a Christian without implications. My new friend avidly read devotions and teachings from other Christian women to boost her faith. It just so happened that I had written some of them.

Our earthly plans are never greater than God's heavenly assignment.

Our meeting was a 1-in-1.2-billion-odds encounter.

That night I couldn't sleep. I went back to that moment when I knew I was supposed to go—in spite of my reservations, in spite of my busy schedule.

He could have picked anyone, but God was showing off in a spectacular way for his daughter who lived in India. A daughter who often felt alone in her faith. A daughter who was fighting cancer. This was never about me.

My assignment had nothing to do with a book launch, a retreat, or whether a trip to India was convenient or not. The Holy Spirit led us three thousand miles to this woman's front door in answer to her prayer. God encouraged her, and I got to be a small part of that.

Not only that, but my suffering years earlier as a young mom with metastatic breast cancer was instrumental in this miracle. God took one of the hardest periods of my life and redeemed it as he comforted and led me to this woman.

As much as I love this story, I still recall times when God took me down a certain path and I didn't have a clue why. I heard the Lord say go, but I didn't see results, not any that would count here on earth. Is it any less Spirit-led when we say yes to the Holy Spirit's direction and there's not a perfect ending to the story? Absolutely not. One day we'll stand in eternity and be surprised at what God was doing. We'll be shocked at the scope of our assignment.

We'll think that we were raising a pack of noisy kids, and he'll show us the "David" in the midst. We'll believe that a waiting time was punishment, and he'll reveal the gift he was trying to give us in that season. We'll look at all our *doing*, and he'll show us how our *being* was the most powerful tool in his hands.

The Word

Those who are led by the Spirit of God are the children of God.

ROMANS 8:14

Your Spirit-Led Promise

You will never wander.

Your Spirit-Led Invitation

Live your assignment, no matter where you are.

Prayer

Holy Spirit, lead me. If fear keeps me from going across the street or across the world, I receive your power to overcome it. If busyness or a crowded schedule keeps me from saying yes, show me what matters to my heavenly Father. I hold up my life to you and receive my assignment, no matter where I am.

5

Hope beyond a Quivering Soul

A Spirit-Led Heart Is
Bold

> God nowhere asks anyone to have a large church. He
> only calls us to do his work, proclaiming his Word to
> people he loves under anointing power of the Holy
> Spirit to produce results that only he can bring about.
>
> Jim Cymbala, *Fresh Wind, Fresh Fire*

"What is the one thing you long for from the Holy Spirit?"

When I asked that question among a group of women on-line, the conversation felt as though a dam had burst. Hopes and insecurities rushed to the surface. There wasn't one woman who didn't desire to be led by the Holy Spirit. There wasn't one woman who didn't long for the Holy Spirit to infiltrate every aspect of her life.

Most admitted the thought was scary.

One friend said, "I pray that God would replace my weak, timid spirit with boldness." She shared that she walked right to the edge of obedience time and time again, only to turn away out of fear. The desire to be in the center of God's will was strong, but apprehension won out most days.

Another said, "I'd love to be able to be like Peter and say, 'I don't have what you need, but I know who does.'" Whether that was a friend going through a tough time, or a stranger whose need was apparent to the whole world, she wanted to settle next to that person and show the love of Jesus, but she didn't know if it would be welcomed. She wasn't sure what to say, so she usually ignored it, all the while her heart tugging her in the opposite direction.

One woman said, "I need courage and bravery that will go beyond my quivering soul." Perhaps this is the one I loved the most. It's a visual of the battle we all face.

In each of these, a thread emerges. We desire boldness in our faith.

Do you relate? I do.

A bold heart is a surrendered heart. You are waving your hand in the air, volunteering for the Holy Spirit to lead you. You are poised on the edge of obedience. You're listening, even in the mundane. You sense that tug, and even when you are unsure of what it looks like, you know God is up to something. You have your game face on and are ready to do whatever is asked of you—until fears creep into that holy moment.

What if I say the wrong thing?

What if they reject me?

What if I . . . ?

If a bold heart is a surrendered heart, you obey even when that makes you feel uncomfortable. You step into the limelight when you really want to hide. A surrendered heart leads you to serve behind the scenes when your flesh longs to be seen and acknowledged for what you do. That Holy Spirit boldness demolishes hindrances between you and a life of surrendered obedience.

The Early Church: Boldness Launches Leaders

In Acts 6 and 7, we find a church experiencing growing pains. Thirty-one years have passed since Jesus's death and resurrection. Some knew Jesus, but many converts have only heard about him. They are compelled by the passion of those who once walked with Jesus.

Don't you love watching new believers grow in their faith?

They are learning to pray. They are discovering faith in Jesus for themselves. They are continually filled with the Holy Spirit and faith and wisdom.

The early church is diverse. It is filled with spiritual babies, spiritual leaders, and everything in between. There is a mix of cultures and backgrounds, including Grecians (Jews who adopted the Greek language and culture), Hebraic Jews, and Gentiles.

The older generation of believers must have looked at this group in awe. There was a time when none of these people would have worked side by side, much less called each other friends.

Growth and diversity are exciting, but they also produce problems. The simple community established by the apostles isn't working any longer. The population of poor and widows has increased, and some accuse the apostles of distributing the fund for their care unequally—that they are giving Hebraic widows the greater share. This is taxing because the apostles are already in a constant tug-of-war for their time and wisdom.

As a leader, it's wise to realize when you can no longer do things on your own or when you've outgrown the old system. The apostles decide to appoint seven elders. They have to be of good reputation, godly, and wise. The new elders will relieve the apostles of the time-consuming tasks of serving the poor and widows and mediating disputes. This leaves the apostles to do what they are called to do—to pray and teach.

They chose Stephen, a man full of faith and of the Holy Spirit; also Philip, Procorus, Nicanor, Timon, Parmenas, and Nicolas from

Antioch, a convert to Judaism. They presented these men to the apostles, who prayed and laid their hands on them.

Acts 6:5–6

Stephen is specially noted as one of the seven. He is described as full of faith and the Holy Spirit. He is trusted for leadership by the people. As one of the first appointed elders in the church, Stephen will "wait on tables" (Acts 6:2). In our culture, that phrase means serving food. Not so in this instance. Stephen and the other six will sit at a table and hear complaints, weigh opinions and make difficult decisions, and disperse funds and food to those who need it. It's a demanding job, but a critical one as the church moves from one growth phase to the next.

Power and grace mark Stephen's life, and they transcend into his new role in ministry. Miracles and wonders take place even as he performs mundane tasks. He continues to teach as well, and one day a niche group of people take notice. Who is this guy "waiting tables" yet so filled with the Holy Spirit? Miracles and wonders follow him, but so do the religious leaders. They listen to him speak and teach. They distract him by arguing with him. He answers with wisdom and discernment, which only frustrates them further. Stephen is quickly seen as a threat. His opposers bribe a few people to spread lies about him. Those false words reach the ears of the Sanhedrin, who are deeply troubled by what they hear.

An outright lie would be disproved immediately. But his accusers have taken a hint of truth and distorted it. They stir and stir until it stinks. Stephen is called to stand before his accusers.

Until now, Stephen has been behind the scenes. He has witnessed the apostles returning from these types of meetings with stripes on their backs. Now it's his turn. He's in trouble. As he stands there, vulnerable, something strange happens. His face shines like the face of an angel (Acts 6:15). What a contrast to the men in front of him! His demeanor is calm. He's composed. He is human, so there is fear, even though he's done nothing wrong. Yet Stephen is so filled with the Holy Spirit that his very stillness and the light coming from within cause them to stare.

This is where boldness is needed.

He's thrust into a choice. He can confess the sins he didn't commit and walk away with a warning. If their accusations stick, at minimum he'll face prison. He'll be tied and beaten. But Stephen opens his mouth and speaks with boldness. His face shining with God's glory, he gives a history lesson detailing God's love toward his people even though they failed him repeatedly. He lists the patriarchs (those whom his accusers adore) and describes how God demonstrated mercy to them, including sending his own son. He speaks of how God continued to reach for his people while they continued to reject him. Point by point, he seeks common ground in shared history. He is unafraid to talk about the parts of history they don't want to hear—how God's people failed him even as he loved them. When he points to the men and describes their role in the death of Jesus, they gnash their teeth like snarling dogs.

Punishment is imminent and Stephen knows it.

"Look," he says. "I see heaven open and the Son of Man standing at the right hand of God" (Acts 7:56).

Stephen is dragged to the edge of the city and they stone him. Even as the stones batter his bones, Stephen looks up into heaven and sees Jesus standing at the right hand of the Father. He points toward the heavens. *Do you see what I see?* With his last breath, Stephen forgives the men responsible.

This feels like the end of Stephen's story.

Just as the Holy Spirit was evident in Stephen's life, he was also present in Stephen's death. His dying words are filled with boldness. No one can deny that something spectacular is taking place, even as he utters his last words.

During the stoning, Stephen's accusers have left their coats at the feet of a man standing in the crowd. The man, who is honored by their actions, is close to the same age as Stephen. If there were a magazine listing the "rising stars" in the ranks of the religious, his face would be on the cover. He describes himself as a Hebrew among Hebrews. He's respected and he is feared. He is zealous in his beliefs and doesn't let anything get in his way.

This is our first time to meet Saul.

He has heard every word Stephen said. He witnesses the young man's glowing face. He sees him point toward the heavens and call out Jesus's name—the very one Saul hates. He listens as Stephen forgives his killers.

Saul goes on a rampage after Stephen's death. He storms from house to house, yanking mothers and fathers from their children because of their faith. He throws believers into prison. Even as he rages, what he witnessed cannot be unseen. It can't be unheard.

Saul pursues those who believe in Jesus, while the one Stephen believed in pursues Saul.

Your Promise: Holy Spirit Boldness Creates a Partnership

A woman stood on her tiptoes, reaching for an item on a top shelf. The guy with her was shorter. He put his arms around her and tried to push her higher. It was almost comical.

"I really want that," I heard her say.

I have long arms. When I was girl, I heard a teacher once comment that she hoped I'd grow into them. After that, I imagined them dragging behind me, like a gorilla's. The rest of me eventually caught up, but my arms are still longer than most. I like that about me. They come in handy, just as they did that day. I reached for the item and scooted it close to the edge with my fingertips. In a couple of seconds, it was in my hands. When I gave it to the woman, she thanked me profusely.

"I really wanted that," she said again.

Remember that conversation I had with my friends about the Holy Spirit and what we longed for most? Most of the women said that they heard or sensed God asking them to take steps of faith, but it felt impossible or overwhelming to do on their own. A Spirit-led heart is a partnership. Paul's second letter to the Corinthian church ends with this blessing:

May the grace of the Lord Jesus Christ, and the love of God, and *the fellowship of the Holy Spirit* be with you all.

2 Corinthians 13:14

The word *fellowship* in this verse comes from the root word *koinōnia*. When Paul wrote this to the church of Corinth, his life had completely transformed. He had become a spiritual father and mentor to the church. He wrote the letters to teach and encourage them in their faith. He wished God's best for them. Grace. God's love. Fellowship (*koinōnia*) with the Holy Spirit.

This partnership was what turned Paul's life around. The love of God gave Paul permission to leave his past behind. Jesus called him to embrace his identity. Fellowship with the Holy Spirit put his feet on a new path and kept them there. It's an image of an active partnership between God the Father, Jesus, and the Holy Spirit in the life of a believer. It takes each of these to live boldly, especially when you are transitioning from "Saul" to "Paul."

We exchange labels for the leading of the Holy Spirit.

I used to allow the label of "introverted" to get in the way of boldness. When I felt God asking me to be bold, I resisted. I didn't mind sharing my opinion, but if boldness meant taking the lead, that's just not who I am.

I'm shy. I'm introverted. I don't make waves.

The "bold" Christians we see in the early church were Spirit-empowered. It didn't have a thing to do with being shy or not shy, introverted or extroverted. They couldn't help but speak of what they had seen and heard (Acts 4:20). Their boldness wasn't arrogant or showy. It was humble and respectful, even when the people opposed them.

We exchange labels for the leading of the Holy Spirit.

Spirit-led boldness reflects the fruit of the Spirit—gentleness, kindness, and self-control.

It is intelligent.

It is courageous.

It is genuine.

It is filled with conviction.

The early church was so convinced about what they were doing that they felt compelled to speak or act. It wasn't driven by emotion or to gain anything from it. When these believers met with adverse reaction, they may have been afraid, but they walked hand-in-hand with courage.

They weren't instruments of controversy, though controversy was sometimes a result.

Boldness means that you are still exactly who God made you to be. Witty. Wise. Funny. Shy. Extroverted. God looks past the label to a surrendered life.

This is where boldness and obedience intersect. If there is a learning curve, it's okay to acknowledge that. If you need a little encouragement, you'll tell those closest to you that you need their prayers. You'll look for encouragement in your relationship with God. Obedience may have you knocking your knees in the beginning, but the more you obey, the more God helps you discover truth that God has always known—about you, about his plans, about trust and dependence that cause your spiritual muscles to strengthen.

The word *koinōnia* is sprinkled throughout the Bible. Let's contrast this fellowship/partnership with doing it in our own strength.

	Koinōnia (fellowship/partnership)	Without fellowship
Acts 2:42	Sharing, bringing resources together	Trying to do it on our own
Romans 15:26	Working together to help others	Trying to fix it on our own
1 Corinthians 1:9	Partnering with Jesus	Trying to figure out what he wants through trial and error
Philippians 2:1–4	Unity	Comparison, competition, isolation

Jesus tells us that he can do nothing on his own (John 5:30). If he is in partnership with his Father and the Holy Spirit, why do we imagine we can do anything without help? Fellowship with the Holy Spirit is partnering with God, for the Holy Spirit reveals the heart of a Father. When we try to fix it, hold it up, or patch it in our own power, he shows us a better way.

Just as Paul prayed over the church of Corinth, we are offered fellowship with the Holy Spirit to have boldness beyond our quivering souls.

Your Invitation: Surrender to the Partnership

Becky is a preschool teacher. We attend church together, and she is part of my Wednesday night Bible study group. She's gracious and quiet and sweet. She is faithful to show up. If she says she's coming, you can count on it. If she's going to be late or unavailable, she gives you plenty of notice. She's a fantastic mom, and she's tearfully cheering her children on as they leave the nest. Becky is a woman making a difference, though her work is not always seen.

One day she and her husband, Dan, were seeking God about their new season as empty nesters. They prayed for God to use their lives however he wished. That's a dangerous prayer, or maybe an adventurous one. The answer came quickly. They both felt the Holy Spirit answer.

Be bolder in your faith.

Maybe, like me, you point to Becky and say, "You are already doing so much."

Becky's prayer wasn't to seek a more public profile or to add to her to-do list. It was a sincere offer to do whatever God wanted her to do. She and Dan were waving a white flag that said, "You're the boss. We surrender to your will."

When Becky shared this story with our group, I asked her where it led her. She laughed. "It led down the dog food aisle." Shortly after that prayer, Becky and her husband were grocery shopping. She passed an employee who had a small cross tacked to his vest.

Talk to him.

The instructions were clear.

Becky is comfortable teaching preschool children. She is comfortable being a mom and loving her children's friends.

Talking to a stranger at a grocery store, not so much.

Her chest fluttered as she approached him. She broke the ice by asking about the cross on his vest. He told her that he and his family had recently moved to the area and were trying to find a new church family. It was a nice conversation. They chatted for a moment and then parted ways. She turned to leave.

Pray for him.

Talking to him was one thing. But praying for him? He was on the clock. They were at the grocery store. The flutter in her chest became a hammer. She wanted to go the other way, except she had prayed and God had asked her to live more boldly.

Let's revisit the definition of that word.

Boldness is a surrendered heart.

She surrendered. Becky turned around and followed the man down the dog food aisle. When she asked if she could pray with him, he said yes. Becky and Dan and the man bowed their heads, moved close, and prayed. There were no other people in the dog food aisle. Only a handful may have noticed, but something sweet and powerful was happening.

The next week the man and his family showed up at Becky's church. He told her that he wanted to be a part of a church where people prayed for you on the spot.

A few Sundays ago I sat behind Becky and Dan in church. When it was time to take communion, they invited me into their circle. I stood with Becky, Dan, Becky's mother, a friend of Dan's from work, and the man they met at the store and his wife. Some were family, but others were a direct result of Becky's being bold.

Since that fateful day, they've shared meals with new friends and spoken into one another's lives.

I asked Becky how comfortable she felt praying in that dog food aisle. She said,

If you had asked me if I felt comfortable before I prayed, I'd say not all, but once I started praying, it felt right. I was exactly where I should be, doing exactly what I was supposed to be doing. To be used of God is humbling, and it's where I want to live.

She believes God set up their meeting and deserves all the credit. Becky believes that if he can use her, he can use anyone. As she describes herself, she's "as ordinary as it gets."

I've never been led to pray for someone at a grocery store, but I have felt God asking me to speak truth to a loved one about Jesus. I've experienced Holy Spirit moments when it was time to go off script in a message and I wanted to resist, because a set of notes you've prepared and prayed over feels a lot safer. When we pray for boldness, we enter fellowship with the Holy Spirit.

We surrender.

We obey even when it's new territory.

We might not see the end of the story. In fact, rarely do we see it. Boldness leads as we become a footnote, a paragraph, or an entire chapter in a story with eternal purpose.

Boldness without borders

By ourselves, we can do nothing.

That's not a weak statement.

When you voice that truth out loud, you surrender to a partnership with God. It turns you in a new direction—that of listening, surrendering, obeying, and absolute fellowship. What a beautiful picture of faith at work in the heart of a believer!

When I don't know what to do, I look to Jesus and I learn from him. During his time on earth, Jesus was in constant fellowship with the Holy Spirit. As I watch his example, it becomes a prayer.

He was led by the Holy Spirit into the wilderness for forty days and forty nights. He walked out overflowing in the Holy Spirit (Luke 4:1–14).

Lord, give us boldness to speak to the enemy in the wilderness. May we be so surrendered to your plan that we walk in filled with the Spirit and walk out just as full.

Jesus was identified by the Holy Spirit (Luke 3:22).

Give me boldness to rest in my identity. To boldly walk into your presence with joy as your beloved daughter. I am marked by you. May I live as if I'm yours.

The Holy Spirit anointed Jesus for ministry (Acts 10:38; Luke 4:18).

I'll go where you ask me to go. I throw up my hands to receive your anointing over my heart, over my home, over my work, and in those private moments when it's just you and me. Fill me up, Holy Spirit. If I start to run on empty, remind me that you are my Source.

Jesus spoke with the power of the Holy Spirit (John 3:34).

When doubt creeps in, may boldness lead me to faith. When I'm put on the spot, I don't have to have all the answers. Help me point back to you with every word, whether I'm talking to a loved one, to a stranger, or on social media. Give me the words you want me to say.

He was resurrected by the Holy Spirit (Romans 8:11).

Lord, I can't even comprehend this. We are promised that the same Spirit that raised you from the dead lives in us. Stir that in my faith. Let me grab hold of it and lean into it. Bring my faith to life with your power. Resurrect those areas in me that have gone dormant.

From his conception until the resurrection, Jesus was in fellowship with his Father and the Holy Spirit. He never tried to do it on his own. That's the message I pray we all grasp. We are in fellowship with the Holy Spirit—in spite of our quivering souls.

The Word

After they prayed, the place where they were meeting was shaken. And they were all filled with the Holy Spirit and spoke the word of God boldly.

ACTS 4:31

Your Spirit-Led Promise

You are in fellowship with the Holy Spirit.

Your Spirit-Led Invitation

Surrender and live your faith more boldly.

Prayer

I surrender to bolder faith. I understand that's not an in-your-face approach, but one that aligns my heart and will with yours in that moment. I am grateful for the love, grace, and fellowship of the Father, Son, and Holy Spirit. What a beautiful picture of my faith in partnership!

6

We Are Worth Fighting For

A Spirit-Led Heart Is Advocated and Comforted

Many people say that the Holy Spirit gives us power,
and that's true, but how does he do that? Does he merely
zap us with higher energy levels? No—by calling him
the *other* Advocate [or Helper], Jesus has given us the
great clue to understanding how the empowering of
the Holy Spirit works. The first Advocate [Jesus] is
speaking to God for you, but the second Advocate [the
Holy Spirit] is speaking to *you* for you.

Tim Keller, *Encounters with Jesus*

Every time I write a book, it seems that I must walk through the
message. This book has been no different. I was on my way to
the airport to return home after a ministry trip when I received a
phone call from my younger daughter, Melissa.

"Have you talked with Leslie?" she asked.

I heard the tears in her voice. "What's going on?"

"The news isn't good, Mom."

A few days earlier, my older daughter, Leslie, had told me that she found a lump. She had promised to make a doctor's appointment as soon as possible. The doctor got her in quickly, and they performed a biopsy. As I talked with Melissa, my phone buzzed. Leslie was calling, so I hung up with one daughter to talk to the other. While Melissa had wept, Leslie's voice was strong. I instantly knew that she was holding herself together for her mom.

"What's up, babe?" I asked.

"It's cancer, Mom. I have an MRI on Monday, but they know for certain it's malignant."

I was on my way home, but still five hours away by air. My friend's husband was driving me to the airport, so it was hard to talk. I told my sweet girl it was going to be all right. I told her I loved her. I told her we'd figure this out together. My friend's husband looked at me when the conversation ended.

"Did you just find out that your daughter has cancer?" he asked incredulously.

I nodded my head yes. Then I climbed out of the car, thanked him for the ride, found an empty bathroom stall in the airport, and wept until I was empty.

Not my baby girl.

Not my sweet girl who climbed in her mama's arms twenty-five years earlier when I was diagnosed with metastatic breast cancer, who held me close and whispered, "Mama, doctors don't know everything."

This battle was all too familiar. Richard had been diagnosed with cancer two years earlier and won that battle. My mom was diagnosed a year later, and we found out just before my ministry trip that she had a recurrence. A few years earlier, I underwent genetic testing when my girls approached the age I had been when I was diagnosed. My results were negative for the gene, and I rejoiced—my daughters should be safe. Now it appeared that, not only was Leslie not safe, but she had taken a direct hit.

I don't know about you, but if you hurt me, I can take it. If you hurt my child, though, it touches the deepest part of me. Everything within me rises up to protect and defend, to keep that child safe.

When we are embattled, the enemy has a plan. He recognizes how vulnerable we are. He moves in while our defenses are down. The plan is to discourage, distract, deceive, or destroy. When the attack is on those we love, we are drawn into that battle. The news of my daughter's unexpected diagnosis made me feel that the enemy was swinging wildly at everything I held precious. I called the friend whose home I had just left. When she heard the news, she promised to pray right then. She texted me two minutes later. "Suzie, when I knelt to pray, the Lord spoke to me. He said, 'Suzie knows what to do.'"

This was confirmation.

When we are in any type of battle, we may identify with the psalmist in Psalm 69:20, who said, "I looked for sympathy, but there was none." The psalmist wasn't looking for pity, but for someone to stand with him in combat. We might change those words to "I looked for strength, and I felt none" or "I looked for answers, and there were none." The core of this cry is that the odds are against us or that we feel alone.

As I sat in that stall in a bathroom in the Phoenix, Arizona, airport, I looked up. The weight of my daughter's diagnosis felt crushing on a mama's heart, but I put my hands in the air. I surrendered to the journey ahead. I prayed for healing. I asked God to show me—beginning in that moment—the goodness of his character and what lessons we would learn together. I asked for wisdom to love my daughter well, as well as her two little girls.

My friend had heard from the Lord, and I believed those words. *I know what to do.*

I know where to turn. I know where my strength lies. In that small bathroom stall in Phoenix, Arizona, this became my psalm: "I looked for help, and you were here."

The Early Church: The Battle Is Real

I am not drawn to movies or books with a fighting theme. I don't like any type of fighting at all, for I am a peacemaker by default. You'll never find me sitting ringside at a boxing match or enjoying the drama of a family fight. Yet there are majestic fighting scenes in the Bible that give us a peek into the spiritual battle going on around us.

In Acts 8 and 9, the enemy is stirring dissension. Saul is creating havoc. He is a zealous and passionate man and believes he is working on the side of God. His presence strikes fear among Christ followers when he strides into a city. Jesus followers hide their children and watch as neighbors and friends are yanked from their homes, imprisoned, and beaten.

They are shaken when friends like Stephen are martyred.

Just after Stephen's death, his friends stand at the brutal scene. His death was unexpected. It was cruel and unjust. Though his last words were glory-filled, who can forget that he was convicted without a trial and buried without ceremony like a common criminal? These same friends now defy authorities and convention to remain at the spot where his body is buried as they mourn him.

Stephen's death is a blow. Going to jail is one thing, but a death by stoning is quite another. Believers begin to scatter for their own protection and for the protection of the church. If you were scoring this round of the fight, it would appear to be a knockout for the enemy—except for this:

> For our struggle is not against flesh and blood, but against the rulers, against the authorities, against the powers of this dark world and against the spiritual forces of evil in the heavenly realms.
>
> Ephesians 6:12

The ongoing battle isn't really about Saul.
Instead, there is a clash in the heavens.

On one side of the ring, the contender holds his hands in the air. He's circling, posturing as if he's greater, bigger. He believes that he is cunning, and he's already acting as if he's the winner.

The one standing on the other side of the ring is meek, but there's no mistaking his strength. He's surrounded by a host of angels. His beauty is not in his countenance, but in his love for humankind. He's fighting not for himself, but for the world. Despised and rejected, he is a man of suffering, familiar with pain. The punishment that brings peace is upon his shoulders, and by his wounds we are healed (Isaiah 53:3, 5).

This battle is the true battle and has already been won.

When we are in a battle, no matter what that looks like, we may feel crushed, bruised, or forsaken. We may feel that we are without help. We may not know how to help ourselves.

We have a Helper!

> In the same way, *the Spirit helps us in our weakness*. We do not know what we ought to pray for, but *the Spirit himself intercedes for us* through wordless groans.
>
> Romans 8:26

It's important to remember in those moments that we have someone fighting on our behalf. We are worth fighting for! The Holy Spirit not only is a Helper, but fights for us in our weakest moments. We'll have plenty to do to meet that battle in the flesh, but he reveals how to combat spiritually. The Spirit of God helps and strengthens us, even when it seems there is no fight left in us. Our opponent may believe he's bigger, yet we are overcomers because of our faith. The Spirit who lives in us is greater than the spirit who lives in the world (1 John 4:4).

You are worth fighting for!

I may not love fighting, but when I found out that my mom and daughter were both battling cancer, I slipped my boxing gloves on as the words that I needed to hear soaked over my hurting soul.

Suz, you know what to do.

We would deal with the obvious emotional and physical issues over the next few months. There would be down moments and down days; however, Jesus made our peace his mission, and when we are in battle, he is in our corner.

God loves us.

Jesus rescues us.

The Holy Spirit brings calm as he equips us for battle.

Your Promise: The Holy Spirit Prepares You for the Fight

My daughter-in-law kickboxes for exercise. Before every class, she wraps her hands in a thin band that protects her tendons and muscles. It keeps her wrists from bending at the wrong angle. These boxing wraps are essential to avoid injury, and it takes time for her to apply them properly. As she wraps, she keeps her wrists straight to avoid wrinkles or gaps. It's time-consuming, but she's at her best when she faces an opponent (or a punching bag).

> And because you belong to him, *the power of the life-giving Spirit has freed you* from the power of sin that leads to death.
>
> Romans 8:2 NLT

Before a battle ever comes, we yield every area of ourselves to the power of the life-giving Spirit. We hold out our hands. We let him wrap them in truth. We ask him to smooth out wrinkles of fear.

We do this whether we are in an apparent battle or not. We have seasons where life runs smooth and the enemy seems to be busy elsewhere. That is often his greatest opportunity. We understand the life-giving power that comes through the Holy Spirit, so we don't wait for the battle. We live this verse: "Since we are living by the Spirit, let us follow the Spirit's leading in every part of our lives" (Galatians 5:25 NLT).

When we do this, we don't have "more" of him—because we already have him in us. We are giving him more of ourselves. When the battle comes, and it will, we have our spiritual gloves on.

He fights for you, to you

A friend and I spoke over the phone. She and her husband felt God calling them to another city. Every time that door opened, something kept them from taking the leap. Unexpected sickness struck their household. A car broke down completely. A struggling child needed to stay in the same place a little longer. A pay cut came just when they needed the funds to make the move. As they prayed, they sensed strongly that God was still asking them to go. Yet they were uncertain of the timing and whether the onslaught of events would ever stop.

As we spoke, my friend said, "Suzie, I'm embarrassed."

"Why?"

"The enemy must know that I'm weak. That's why we are under such persecution."

Do you know the holy anger that fires up in you when you know that someone is accusing or lying to someone you care about? That's what blazed inside of me. Not at her, but at an enemy who lies to us. This is a close friend, and I knew that she would not take my words as a rebuke.

"You don't get to do that," I said, tears brimming.

"What, Suzie?"

"You're being 'Job's friend' to yourself. It's incredibly unfair to you."

Job was a man who lost everything. His friends came to "cheer" him up in his lowest hour. They started out well. They sat with him in his misery (Job 2:11–12). Then they detoured. They blamed Job, saying he must have done something wrong to bring such tragedy his way (Job 4). Job chastened his friends, but so did God on his behalf.

After the Lord had said these things to Job, he said to Eliphaz the Temanite, "I am angry with you and your two friends, because you have not spoken the truth about me, as my servant Job has."

Job 42:7

God emphasizes that when we blame ourselves for the enemy's attack, we are also not speaking the truth about him. That's weighty. It's hard enough to suffer the words of an insensitive friend, but how many times do we put on the boxing gloves and beat ourselves up? Whether it is a personal, spiritual, or emotional battle, the Holy Spirit is our Advocate. One of the most powerful ways that he fights for us is when he steps into the battle of our thoughts and redirects misguided blame. Tim Keller describes the Helper's role of Advocate (fighter) beautifully: "The first Advocate [Jesus] is speaking to God for you, but the second Advocate [the Holy Spirit] is speaking to *you* for you."[1]

It's a one-two punch.

Jesus fights for you in the presence of God. Then the Holy Spirit goes to work, stepping into the fight raging in your thoughts. He reminds you of who you are. He lets you know that the Lord of Hosts is on your side.

My friend is a warrior. She's a fierce, faith-filled woman, mother, and wife. She's talented and creative. Yet the enemy had lied, telling her that her battle was her fault.

Why?

Because she is a threat to his plans; she walks, lives, and breathes her faith. Her external battle is heavy, but her inner battle was her biggest threat. The fact that she was beating herself up when she needed encouragement and truth only made her burden heavier.

Perhaps you identify. The loudest incrimination often comes from within.

Why am I in this battle?
Did I do something wrong?
Am I weak?
Shouldn't I feel stronger/bigger/badder?

Is God mad at me?

When Jesus used the word *advocate* to describe the Holy Spirit in John 14:16, it was a promise that the Holy Spirit will fight alongside Jesus. He makes the presence of Christ so vibrant that we sense him fighting for us before the Father. Meanwhile, the Helper teaches. He brings to memory fighting words from Scripture that confound and confront the enemy. He brings clarity to the battle. Our lives bear witness to our faith over our circumstances.

The battle may feel chaotic, but the Helper brings clarity.

The Greek word for *advocate* is *paraclete*. It describes the Holy Spirit as both our Advocate and our Comforter. It means the Holy Spirit is "called to our side." It's like having a legal defense who intercedes for us. The Holy Spirit knows who we are. He knows the love the Father has toward us. He puts on boxing gloves and swipes away the untruthful thoughts we speak to ourselves. He's sent from the Father on our behalf and is positioned for the fight. His fists are drawn. His stance is firm, but also compassionate.

If you are in a battle, consider who is fighting on your side.

The Holy Spirit is your Advocate. Will you allow him to fight for you?

Do you believe you are worth fighting for?

Your Invitation: Allow the Holy Spirit to Fight through You

Stephen was martyred, which might make us believe that he lost the fight. What we don't see (and Stephen had a glimpse of it) was the eternal triumph. This is where we are tempted to falter. We see only what is in front of us, but God sees from a greater vantage. When Stephen was martyred, the church was battered. Believers ran for safety. Philip, one of the seven chosen to serve with Stephen, was among the men who scattered. After Stephen's death, he fled to Samaria. He couldn't see the future. He wasn't sure where he would eventually land.

So he kept doing what he was called to do.

He told the Samaritans about Jesus. Wonders and miracles accompanied his testimony. Unclean spirits fled, and the lame and paralyzed were healed. When the apostles heard of the events in Samaria, Peter and John hustled to assist Philip. The believers had been baptized in water to symbolize their new faith, but there was one more gift to receive. The apostles laid hands on the Samaritans, and they were filled with the Holy Spirit. Revival broke out in Samaria!

What the enemy meant for harm, God used to fuel and enlarge the church.

When we are in a battle, we keep doing what we know to do.

After I found out that my daughter had cancer, my friend's words to me, *"God said, 'Suzie knows what to do,'"* rang in my head over and over the next several months. I heard them when I found out my daughter's surgery would take eight hours. I heard them when I was holding one of her girls, who was confused when her mom wasn't able to hold her in those first weeks after surgery. I couldn't fix the situation, but that didn't mean I was powerless.

I was worth fighting for, and so was my daughter.

I could pray. I could be present. I could make freezer meals that she could prepare easily. I could remember to laugh. I could accept help and prayer support of kind friends, who held my arms up while I held up my daughter's.

If I believe that I'll step onto the battlefield every time I write a book, the temptation is to do something different. Maybe I should write *Potty Training Made Easy in Three Steps.* That would be a bestseller, right? It would be no threat at all.

If I knew three easy steps to potty training I would have tried them when my own children were young. More importantly, it's not what God has asked me to do. I'm a Bible teacher and encourager. He's called me to come alongside women and teach about Jesus.

We will have trials.

We will encounter obstacles.

We will face hardship.

There's no promise of an easy life, but there is a promise of a full and abundant life. That unfolds in every part of your life, even the harder parts. Your life is full because you are doing what God has called you to do, whether that's being a mom or a friend, loving others, or making a difference in your community. Your life matters to God, and so do the lives of others. We are all part of an eternal plan to make a difference in the world, and God has a way of using our hardest experiences for his greatest triumphs.

When Philip arrived in Samaria, it was an opportunity for him to hide. He could have given up. He could have gone back to his old profession or quietly lived his faith in a way that made no waves.

He didn't, because it wasn't in him.

He was persecuted, but he was still Philip.

He still played a part in the church. Jesus's instructions to "go into the world" hadn't disappeared because of a battle.

The Holy Spirit was fighting for Philip.

He was fighting *to* Philip.

He was also fighting through him.

Philip was in an unfamiliar place, but his message was still planted in those around him. Wonders and miracles still occurred. People were intrigued by the Word of God, but they were also intrigued by this man who lost a friend and who had to run for his life but still passionately spread the gospel. Philip lived the words that Paul would one day speak, saying we are "persecuted, but not forsaken; struck down, but not destroyed" (2 Corinthians 4:9 NKJV).

Some naysayers maintain that if God loved us, we'd never have to stand on the front lines. But we all stand on the front lines at some point in our lives.

The difference is that we don't stand alone.

Our purpose isn't diminished by the battle, and it may very well be illuminated through it.

Spirit-Led Advocacy without Borders

When we realize we are worth fighting for, we begin to fight for others. That's a game changer. When people go through incredibly hard things, we pull on our spiritual boxing gloves and step into the ring with them.

> Praise be to the God and Father of our Lord Jesus Christ, the Father of compassion and the God of all comfort, who comforts us in all our troubles, so that we can comfort those in any trouble with the comfort we ourselves receive from God. For just as we share abundantly in the sufferings of Christ, so also our comfort abounds through Christ.
>
> 2 Corinthians 1:3–5

We are familiar with a particular battle and are on the other side. We draw close to others who are in their own airport bathroom stall, weeping. The very things that the enemy once meant for harm in our lives become Spirit-led comfort to others.

A young woman recently asked me, "If God is so powerful, why do so many suffer?"

In her honest question, I heard three things:

- Does God care?
- Why bother with faith?
- If only God would do something.

Does God care?

Some have more than enough food. Others go without.

More than 50 percent of the world's female population is oppressed. Women are denied rights that we take for granted.

While some children grow up in a caring home, others do not.

Does God care about this? He does. Jesus drew children close. He knelt to speak to the oppressed. He took the sins of the world upon himself. He instructed believers to care for the orphaned and widowed among them.

A few years ago, a study found that hunger is caused by poverty and inequality, not scarcity.

> For the past two decades, the rate of global food production has increased faster than the rate of global population growth. The world already produces more than 1 ½ times enough food to feed everyone on the planet. That's enough to feed 10 billion people, the population peak we expect by 2050.[2]

My cabinets are full. I throw away food when it passes the expiration date or when the banana is too ripe. We have such an abundance of food in our society, it's easy to overindulge. It's easy to forget that millions of people go hungry every day.

God cares, but what is our response? Are we fighting for those who lack?

Let's speak on their behalf. Let's give to reputable organizations that are making a difference. Let's ask for justice. Let's be that justice.

This is what we discussed when the young woman asked her question about suffering. I'm not sure if this was the answer she expected, but it's something we need to talk about.

Read the words Jesus so passionately shared in Luke 4:18–19. He was sent to heal the brokenhearted, loose the prisoner, set free the oppressed, and offer good news to those impoverished in spirit and otherwise. Jesus pursued that mission so passionately that there were days he was exhausted physically, but he continued to pray and do the work of his Father all the way to the cross.

God has done and is doing his part because he cares.

What might it look like if the church (all of us) did the same?

Why bother with faith?

When problems seem too big, our tendency is to say, "Why bother?" After all, what can we do? Though we aren't asked to be Jesus, we can be his hands and feet. Even as I write that, it feels trite, but it's true.

When I found out my mom and daughter were both fighting cancer, friends and strangers stepped in. Some sent cards. Some sent gift cards for meals. Some cooked. One friend came by a week after Leslie's surgery and blow-dried and fixed her hair. This was awesome, because I discovered that I am the worst at fixing hair. She made Leslie feel beautiful after extensive surgery, when she couldn't do that personal task on her own.

We think that we have to make grand gestures, and sometimes that's exactly where God might lead. For most of us, though, it's the small things that make the biggest difference.

When we become world-changing, Spirit-led fighters in ways big or small, it shows the person we've reached out to that he or she is valued by God.

It's not about the size of what we do, but about being open to the leading of the Holy Spirit.

If only God would do something.

God has already done all that we need by sending his son, but he continues to love.

In love, he asks that his people live their faith.

We love our faith. We love that it comforts us. We love that God is present. We love the power of Scripture in our own lives. We love community.

But living it can be sacrificial too.

It might be buying less so that we can give more, and doing it privately. Maybe it's speaking up on behalf of a child who is bullied, or opening your home to a teenager who is a little bit of a mess but needs to know that Jesus loves him. It might be taking someone to church who doesn't have a car.

It might be giving a little bit more grace to ourselves.

In each situation, we put on our spiritual boxing gloves, and the Helper climbs in the ring.

He marches in and shows us that person, that event, that situation through God's perspective. He invites us to view the battle eternally.

This is not a do-more teaching. If that is what you are feeling right now, rebuke that thought. He doesn't ask us to save the world, because that's not our job. That job has already been filled beautifully. He simply asks us to believe that God cares, that faith matters, and that when we respond as the church, it's transformative.

If we live long enough, we'll be on both sides of the battle.

We'll be the one needing an advocate. We'll be the one who serves as an advocate. In both, a Spirit-led heart is empowered with inner strength through "glorious, unlimited resources" (Ephesians 3:16 NLT).

Currently, I'm on the receiving side. I know that it is a temporary battle. I don't want to be in it, but I'm thankful. There is comfort. There are people fighting with us. There is surprising joy in unexpected moments when I feel God's presence close. There is trust as I ask God to show me the miracles that only he can produce in times like these.

Whatever our battle looks like, I am worth fighting for. And so are you.

The Word

Take the helmet of salvation and the sword of the Spirit, which is the word of God. And pray in the Spirit on all occasions with all kinds of prayers and requests. With this in mind, be alert and always keep on praying for all the Lord's people.

EPHESIANS 6:17-18

Your Spirit-Led Promise

The Holy Spirit fights for you, *to* you.

Your Spirit-Led Invitation

Allow the Holy Spirit to fight for you and for others.

Prayer

I'm worth fighting for. Just saying those words breaks something in me, Father. Your greatest work in me can be produced in my greatest battles. Start in my thought life as you fight for me, to me. As I put on spiritual gloves, may I do so knowing that my first move is toward you. In Jesus's name, amen.

That one is worth fighting for, Lord. I am not big enough to change the world on my own, but I can do my part. Open her eyes. Let her know she is of value to you. Show me how to come alongside and love in your name. Amen.

7

We Will Know What to Do

A Spirit-Led Heart Is Counseled

One of the greatest thrills of my life has been completely depending on God when no human help was available or capable of solving the problem.

Evelyn Christenson,
What God Does When Women Pray

We hiked up the gorgeous trail. Red and yellow fall leaves fluttered from trees trying to hang on to the last drop of summer. Up, up, up we went. My legs ached. I could only imagine how it stretched the legs of the two little guys behind me. The three-year-old and five-year-old started the hike with energy and enthusiasm, which was now clearly lagging. I turned around to check on them. The three-year-old lay crumpled in a heap.

His parents made it to him before I did, and his mother cradled him in her lap.

"Are you tired?" she asked.

"You left me!" he wailed.

He had lost sight of them for a second, and that was enough to frighten him. They had their eyes on him the whole time, but he didn't know that. His dad picked him up from his mom's arms and held him close. I heard him whisper, "Son, I will never leave you. I promise you that. I will always know where you are and how to find you. If you think you are lost, just stop. Don't move even a step, and I'll come to you as quick as I can."

As I watched, I couldn't help but think of my heavenly Father. There have been seasons that I've been plowing along, and suddenly I feel uncertain. It feels as though God is a million miles away. I know he's near, but I can't feel him. I can't touch him. As this earthly daddy spoke soothing words over his little guy's heart, I thought of all the times that God showed up in my lonely places of uncertainty. I imagined my heavenly Father kneeling beside me in those crumpled-on-the-ground moments. I sensed his words deep in my soul.

If you think you are lost, Suzie, just stop.

Don't keep going.

I know right where to find you.

From the beginning, the mission of the Father was intimacy with his creation. He longs to talk to us. He longs to show us what to do, to unfold his plans in our lives. We are never so lost or uncertain that we cannot be found.

The Early Church: Knowing What To Do

Up till now, we've studied what the Holy Spirit *is*. His attributes. His character. Now we transition to what we are *not* because he is our Counselor. We are not orphaned, abandoned, or left behind.

In this next portion of Acts, there are drastic changes. Saul is no longer a threat. He had been on his way to Damascus when he heard a voice from heaven. A blinding light stunned him and took his sight. He made a turnaround. Saul the tormentor became Paul the apostle. He has joined the church he had previously wronged, and with the same zeal he used to have in tormenting believers, he now is intent on spreading the gospel. The apostles have reservations about the authenticity of his conversion at first, but it doesn't take long to see that he is a different man.

He is also part of God's overall plan to love the world.

Before Paul's conversion, the early church almost could have been viewed as a Jewish sect. But Paul's primary call will be to Gentiles (Acts 13:47). This is tricky, because there is deep prejudice between Jews and Gentiles, and it's gone on for generations. The apostles have stayed on one side of that dividing line for the most part, even though Jesus had steered them over it many times. Traditions and cultural worldview have a way of creating margins—even when it contradicts what Jesus modeled.

One night Peter has a vision.

A sheet is lowered to earth by four corners. It's filled with animals that are not allowed in any Jewish person's diet—including reptiles and birds. In the vision, a voice instructs Peter to kill the animals and eat the meat. Though he believes this to be the voice of the Lord, it contradicts what Peter has been taught over the years.

"Surely not, Lord!" Peter replied. "I have never eaten anything impure or unclean." The voice spoke to him a second time, "Do not call anything impure that God has made clean." This happened three times, and immediately the sheet was taken back to heaven.

Acts 10:14–16

When we read this story, we might condemn Peter. He's arguing with God! How much more convincing does a person need?

We could condemn Peter, but if we do, we have to look at ourselves first.

How many times does our lack of understanding get in the way? Perhaps a doctrinal teaching contradicts God's Word, yet we buy in because people we respect speak it. Cultural standards lead away from biblical truth, but we still wrestle because it's isolating when we believe one way and the rest of the world looks at it differently.

What about those times that God asks us to do something new, but we hold on to the old because it's familiar?

What about that time God asks us to love someone, but we worry about what others might think?

These are only a few of the struggles.

Each leaves us feeling a little lost. A little apprehensive. We point to Peter and say, "Why are you arguing with God?" and forget how many times we have done it ourselves because we simply didn't know what to do.

The Counselor not only knows the plans of the Father, but searches to find our part in it.

> For God has unveiled them and revealed them *through the [Holy] Spirit; for the Spirit searches all things [diligently]*, even [sounding and measuring] the [profound] depths of God [the divine counsels and things far beyond human understanding].
>
> 1 Corinthians 2:10 AMP

God wakes up Peter with a vision because he is also a part of God's plan. As a leader, Peter will need to get on board with Paul ministering to Gentiles.

It's not the first time Peter has heard this message. Jesus broke cultural boundaries often. He ate dinner with a tax collector and his friends. He touched the skin of a leprous man. He offered women dignity in a culture that equated them with dogs. Jesus crossed barriers because he saw people rather than taboos. Peter witnessed it all. He was right beside Jesus, but has been holding on to tradition. If Peter is to walk through an open door of God's plan, his closed mind has to be addressed.

Author Gregg Levoy believes that our "callings keep surfacing until we deal with them."[1]

God is gracious enough to speak until we listen—or until we firmly shut the door to God's plan for us through disobedience.

God speaks to Peter three distinct times in the vision—even as Peter argues with him. It is Peter's turn to listen or not.

Your Promise: He Speaks to You

Peter hears a knock at the front gate. Three men have been sent by Cornelius, a Gentile centurion.

Cornelius has sought the Lord in prayer. He had his own vision, which has led him to Peter. The three messengers tell Peter that Cornelius needs to see him. The next morning, they travel to Cornelius's home. When he arrives, Peter makes this declaration:

> "You know it is against our law for a Jewish man to enter a Gentile home like this or to associate with you. But God has shown me that I should no longer think of anyone as impure or unclean."
>
> Acts 10:28 NLT

There it is. His prejudices are front and center. He admits them, but he also admits that he's wrong in those prejudices. He's conflicted but open.

Peter would have hesitated to follow the men to Cornelius's house if not for the dream.

When Cornelius shares his own vision, the divide crumbles. He clearly sees that God shows no favoritism, and he starts preaching.

> While Peter was still speaking these words, *the Holy Spirit came on all* who heard the message. The circumcised believers who had come with Peter were astonished that the *gift of the Holy Spirit had been poured out even on Gentiles.* For they heard them speaking in tongues and praising God.
>
> Then Peter said, "Surely no one can stand in the way of their being baptized with water. *They have received the Holy Spirit* just as we have." So he ordered that they be baptized in the name of Jesus Christ. Then they asked Peter to stay with them for a few days.
>
> Acts 10:44–48

Revival breaks out in a Gentile centurion's home. All are saved. All are filled. All are baptized to signify that they are followers of Jesus.

Sometimes we don't know what we don't know.

This is why we desperately need a Counselor. We all have gaps when it comes to faith. We all have gaps when it comes to God's plans for our church, our family, our marriage, our nation, our lives. We come to faith as babes, and we grow. At some point we transition from the bottle to spiritual meat. We practice our faith and we live it. In every part of this we need counsel—advice, guidance, insight.

> *Sometimes we don't know what we don't know.*

We don't know what we don't know, but the Holy Spirit knows.

Your Invitation: Sit with the Ultimate Counselor

I'm married to a licensed professional counselor. He's a wise and funny man who works primarily with children. The back of his Prius is filled with games, puppets, and sand tray toys. He meets with children at their schools, in their homes, or in his office if a parent or guardian can bring them. In his office, his shelves are filled with therapy playthings. Our grandson Luke doesn't know exactly what his "Big Dad" does, but he tells everyone he's a toy expert.

It's pretty great having a counselor as a husband, except for when he tries to counsel me.

One day Richard and I were talking, and he said, "Okay, Suzie. What I heard you say was . . ."

I laughed. "Uh-uh. No way, mister. What you heard me say was exactly what came out of my mouth. You don't get to be a therapist right now, just my husband."

While I love to tell that story tongue in cheek, I admit there's a benefit to being in close proximity with a counselor, whether you are related or not. Counselors value the importance of listening.

They care more about the person sitting in front of them than about being right. They ask questions, which is a great tool.

An earthly counselor helps with two things. The first is to discover the *why* behind behavior. An earthly counselor will gently refocus attention from the *what* to the *why*. We get so focused on what we are doing that we fail to explore why. If we understand why we do what we do, we are free to change direction.

The second is to change the way we respond. Most of us react rather than respond. Good counsel allows us to respond with our brains rather than with emotion. We think through a situation. We see the other person standing in front of us. We dig deeper to the real issue instead of focusing on the momentary blast of feelings.

Then we can reframe our thinking.

The missing pieces start to fall in place, and our perspective changes. It leaves room for things like compassion, setting healthy boundaries, or seeing ourselves through God's eyes—not that failed relationship, a past choice, or the words of a broken person.

Combined, this is powerful!

We consider the why, which alters our response and changes the way we think—which changes our lives.

If an earthly counselor can help us do that, what can the ultimate Counselor do in our spiritual lives?

"No eye has seen, no ear has heard, and no mind has imagined what God has prepared for those who love him."

1 Corinthians 2:9 NLT

This is what we discover through the Counselor. God reveals these things through his Spirit. When Peter had the vision, God used it to strip away prejudices that stood in the way of Peter's growth process. They were so deeply ingrained that he couldn't remove them on his own.

The Lord started with the why.

Peter, this is why you believe the way you do.

He challenged age-old beliefs and built-in resistance. Peter's vision was a glimpse into the heart of our heavenly Father. The Lord spoke to Peter three times in this vision, giving him the opportunity to respond rather than have the same old reaction. Gregg Levoy talks about the effectiveness of this type of repetition:

> In the Bible, God often called to the prophets by repeating their names twice. "Abraham, Abraham." "Jacob, Jacob." "Moses, Moses." Once, it seems, wasn't enough. Indeed, repetition is fundamental to learning. Ask teachers, ask advertisers, ask parents. "Still, small voices" may not have enough voltage to rattle the status quo, but they do have staying power.[2]

In partnership with our Counselor, God keeps speaking until we hear him. He opens our eyes to what we don't know. As we respond to him, we become teachable. Moldable. Open to the new. Our eyes are opened, slowly at first, but continually until we see. Wisdom and insight fill gaps a bit at a time.

When God speaks through the Counselor, it isn't a rebuke, but a call to growth. He graciously reveals how a lack of knowledge might limit us in a specific area. This changes the way we perceive those things or that person, which alters our response—which has the power to transform the way we love and live our faith.

Our relationship with the Counselor is a two-way conversation. Let's explore a few ways that he speaks and how to listen.

He speaks directly

A friend was in trouble and I didn't know how to help. She had been doing well as a new believer but had fallen back into an old behavior. This damaged an already fragile relationship with a loved one. I lay in bed praying. My prayers were borne out of a desire to help my friend, but the words that bubbled out of my mouth were out of desperation rather than faith.

It's the fixer that lives in me!

I asked God what *I* could do, what *I* should say, how *I* could make things better for her. If you had asked me, I would have told you I was praying for my friend. Not really. I was worrying out loud.

I sensed that voice, the one that has become familiar over the years.

Suzie, what did I ask you to do?

To teach your Word and to love her, Lord.

Are you doing that?

I am.

Let me be God, and you just keep doing what I've asked you to do.

The words weren't audible, but they were from him. They spoke directly to my angst and to the situation. It redirected my prayers from how to fix her to the belief that God loves her. It also relieved me of a burden I wasn't asked to carry. I am her friend, but I'm not powerful enough to make everything right again. God might ask me to do or say something to encourage her, but it would be Holy Spirit–directed rather than a production of worry.

When we stop trying to fix someone, we open our own hearts to transformation.

We might be trying so hard or saying so much that our chatter is louder than the voice of God in their ears. When we pause to consider the counsel of the Holy Spirit, what we don't know is balanced with what God already sees.

How will we know if it's the Holy Spirit?

When Saul heard Jesus's voice on the road to Damascus, he asked, "Who are you, lord?" (Acts 9:5 NLT). Saul didn't know who was speaking. Some translations of Scripture capitalize *Lord* in this verse, while others lowercase it or use the more generic *sir*. All Saul knew was that this was something or someone far bigger than he.

Perhaps, like Saul, you wonder how to distinguish the voice of God from all the other voices that we hear. We can trust in these guidelines:

- The Holy Spirit will never contradict God's Word.
- The Holy Spirit won't appease our hearts to defy the Father's.
- The Holy Spirit is tenacious. In his mercy, he wakes us at night, finds us where are hiding, speaks into our disobedience, gently nudges and tugs, and offers a right-now word that leads, directs, comforts, encourages, or points to understanding that isn't there in the natural.

As in any conversation, we have free will to listen or join in. We can disobey, ignore, or run from his voice, even to the point where it is muffled because we refuse to hear. We are given a choice to continue on in our limited understanding, but why would we?

When we listen, the Holy Spirit moves us beyond our own understanding (2 Peter 1:21). We see it differently. We stop carrying a burden of "what if." This doesn't mean a situation will magically disappear, but we gain the tools we need.

He speaks through others

A particular message—a specific promise for my life—has been spoken over me four separate times by four different people who don't know each other. This is not something that happens to me on a regular basis, and at first I wasn't sure what to do about it. I've only shared it with my husband. This message is tucked away like a precious heirloom. I believe I'll receive the promise, but I can't make it happen on my own. I'd be out of God's will if I tried.

When we receive this type of word from someone, it can be humbling. It can also be confusing, especially when they say it's from God.

How do we know what is truth and what is not?

Peter had heard directly from the Lord, but God used Cornelius to verify that message.

When the first person shared this message with me, it confirmed what God had already spoken to me through the Holy Spirit. All the messages came from people I trusted, or at least felt peace about as they shared.

If we are unsure of a message (or the person delivering it), we pray about it. We can write it down and tuck it away, even if only for a few hours. When the Holy Spirit spoke through an angel to Mary, she pondered it. This means she didn't rush out and tell the world that she was going to be the mother of the Messiah. She weighed it. She held it close and gave it space to breathe. Later, she shared her news with a trusted relative and with those closest to her.

If you are told that God spoke but it contradicts Scripture, or there's a strong "This isn't from God" response from the Holy Spirit, thank the person and move on.

Why does God use people? Because sometimes we have trouble hearing him. He speaks, but if there's a price to pay, we may need to hear the words out loud. In Peter's vision, God spoke three times, but Cornelius confirmed it. There was a price to pay for eating unclean foods (even though God said they were now clean) and hanging out with Gentiles. Peter would receive criticism for going to a Gentile's home, so this particular message wasn't easy to receive.

Later, when Peter told his closest friends what had taken place, they rebuked him just as he had anticipated: "You entered the home of Gentiles and even ate with them!" (Acts 11:3 NLT).

Criticism had the power to discourage Peter, but it didn't. He had been assured that this was from God. He explained how the Holy Spirit had led him to Cornelius. He told them how the Holy Spirit had fallen on everyone in Cornelius's home and filled them. His friends not only believed Peter, but became pivotal figures in this new adventure. They bought into God's plan as well.

Has God been speaking to you through his Holy Spirit?

Is he leading you in a new direction?

Are you listening?

If you've been resisting, stop and ask why. Perhaps if you show love to that difficult person or take that leap of faith, you'll be criticized. Knowing *why* you are struggling helps you to see the bigger picture. Express your hesitation, but listen to the voice of the Holy Spirit. Open your ears to what God is trying to show you.

There's a plan. With God, there's always a plan!

Peter's willingness to listen led Cornelius to salvation, along with his entire household (Acts 11:14). This started a spiritual healing among people who had been divided for centuries. It broadened the reach of the church. It further validated the cross, for Jesus came so that all might be saved.

As I hold these four separate words from God (all saying the same thing), I remember this:

- If God is speaking, then he'll do what he says he'll do.
- I can't make it happen, but I can prepare for it spiritually and emotionally.
- My waiting time allows me to seek the eternal viewpoint in it (the why).

If he spoke it long ago and it hasn't happened yet, don't let go. Hold it close. Be open to what he's doing in you now—which might be instrumental later. Take steps as the Holy Spirit directs, and wait with an expectant heart.

He speaks through the Word

The Bible is God's heart, but too often the Bible is our last resort. Or maybe that's just me. I clean the house, pay bills, cook dinner, scroll through social media, run through my work tasks, and do a hundred different things every single day. Sitting to read the Bible may get put to last place, even though I love the Word.

There's a reason we struggle.

There's life between the pages, and the last thing the enemy wants is the body of Christ to live in the Word. The last thing he wants is for you and me to understand what we are missing.

In C. S. Lewis's classic allegory *The Screwtape Letters,* a demon instructs an underling how to distract and distort faith in the heart of a believer. In one scene, he says,

> It is funny how mortals always picture us as putting things into their minds: in reality our best work is done by keeping things out.[3]

He was referring to the Word. If we make studying the Word one more chore, we aren't losing a day in our reading plan, we are running on empty.

Our Counselor uses the Word. He dips into the reservoir of the Word we pour over our heart as if it's living water.

If you wrestle with reading the Word, you aren't alone. So let's put the guilt aside and be honest about the fact that it doesn't always come easily. There are many aspects of our faith that come with built-in spiritual resistance. Prayer is one of them. Obedience is another. Forgiveness is a big one. Reading the Word is one of our most potent battlegrounds.

Recognizing this allows me to skip the guilt and see time studying the Word as a prize worth pursuing.

Imagine that you are hungry, exhausted, and wilting. There's a table filled with prepared food, and nearby a comfortable bed and a steaming bath are waiting just for you. In the natural, you'd sit at that table and nourish your body. You'd eat every bite and scoop the last drop of deliciousness out of the bowl. You'd slip into the tub with bubbles and hot water and soak until all your aches and pains subsided. You'd climb into that California king bed, pull the thick cover up to your chin, and sleep for eight blissful hours.

We pour out every day, leaving most of us spiritually hungry and overstretched, our souls dry as a bone. If we recognize the Word as our source of spiritual food, rest, and renewal, it changes the way we approach studying the Word. We recognize the battle—and bust the barriers.

First, we find our rhythm. Not too long ago I stayed overnight with my sister. My brother was also in town. The three of us were up early, while other family members slept in. I waltzed into the kitchen singing a soft tune. My sister and brother gave me the evil eye.

"I haven't had coffee yet," my sister said.

"Morning people," my brother muttered.

We all have parts of our day that are our best. My sister loves to tuck in with the Word in the evening. I'm not really a morning person, though I'm not as cranky as some. I'm best midmorning, so I've learned to tackle all the nonthinking tasks before then. Around ten o'clock is a sweet time to worship and read and study. It launches the rest of my workday as I write, prepare messages, blog, and take care of details. It's my rhythm, and if I force myself to pray and study at night or to do it first thing in the morning (because I think it's more spiritual to do it at five a.m.), it's not the same.

I talk to God all day long, but I meet with him most days at ten a.m.

What is your rhythm?

First, invite the Lord into it. God doesn't define a portion of the day as more holy; he simply delights in the fellowship of his daughter.

Second, introduce quiet so that you can hear the Word. Silence is a fading art. It may be harder for some of you than others due to your current season of life. For example, it's easier for my mom to find quiet than it is for me, and it's easier for me to find quiet than it is for those surrounded by little people.

For some, quiet is shutting down outside noise. I struggled to hear the voice of the Holy Spirit for a season. I prayed about that and saw an image of me with my phone in my hand. As it is for many people, my phone is my calendar, my connection to a lot of people (or I imagine it to be), my digital map, and access to email, texts, and social media. I read books on it. It's my camera. It's my entertainment.

It's all those things, but it's not my God.

My phone is a great technological tool, and it makes my life easier in several ways. Yet I had left no room for quiet because it was in my hand for most of the day and into the evening. I could pretend this isn't a battle for me, but if I want to hear the voice of the Holy Spirit, I'm going to admit it.

I realized that I kept it close wherever I was. I reached for it even when there wasn't something pressing. I was out of balance. It was robbing me of quiet. If the Holy Spirit wanted my attention, he had to shout over social media and the lastest ping on my phone.

I'd love to say that I put it down without a fight, but it took time. It's still a temptation, but it's not the boss of me. I pursue quiet as I intentionally place the phone in the other room or shut it off completely at a certain time of the day. I use it to answer a phone call in the evening hours, but it's not my life.

Never let anyone's voice be louder in your ear than God's.

I gave myself permission to hear the voice of God.

I confessed that there are times I give my phone more say than the voice of the Holy Spirit.

I know this is an area where I need to be vigilant. There is no voice that should be louder than God's in my life.

Is there anything that has greater volume in your own life?

Pause for a moment and ask the Counselor to show you what that is. As he reveals it, praise God for the insight. When we know what we are battling, change begins.

Giving ourselves permission for quiet leaves more room for the Word. It gives space to read books that feed our soul and draws us deeper into Scripture and our relationship with God. That's not going to look the same for everyone. When I had three little ones under the age of three, quiet was a bath. When I commuted to a job, quiet was my time in the car.

As we read the Word, we ask the Holy Spirit to illuminate it (Ephesians 1:18). The Holy Spirit delves beneath that cloud that has been hanging over us to reveal the beauty of what is unseen. As we read, it becomes a conversation with God as the Holy Spirit brings it to life.

Ponder Scripture rather than pounding out a reading schedule.

Spend as much time as you need on a passage of Scripture. Ask questions. You may spend a week on one passage, but you'll walk away understanding it. That's better than reading ten chapters and having no idea what you just consumed.

We are invited to sit with the Counselor.

Our Spirit-led heart begins to see what we couldn't before. We respond to God's leading and to the counsel of the Holy Spirit. We respond, whether in obedience or acceptance, and the way we believe or think shifts. We delight in what we've learned or are learning. The narrow constraints put on us are unshackled.

Whatever he's asking, we say yes. If there's new territory ahead, we are unafraid to explore it.

Counseling without Borders

An earthly counselor loves nothing more than working with someone who shows up ready to work. The person sitting across from them is a work-in-progress and admits it. They are tired of putting the blame on others, because it's gotten them nowhere. They don't have all the answers, but they are open to finding them. Growth is ahead. This might expose gaps that need to be filled, but that's exciting rather than intimidating.

A few years ago, an extended family member admitted that alcohol had bullied him for way too long. He was tired of the cycle of drinking, and tired of the consequences. He called to ask for help, and Richard recommended a place where he could go.

He was desperate and broken. His life was tumbling down around him, but going for help was inconvenient. Costly. It meant telling the world that he couldn't do this on his own. Regardless, he drove himself to the facility the next morning and sat on a park bench for an hour before it opened.

He checked himself in, and we didn't hear from him for six weeks.

"Is he going to be okay?" I asked my husband.

Richard smiled. "Anyone who asks for help and then listens and responds like he did has a really great chance of a new life. I think he's going to be okay."

It's been a few years.

That loved one is still free.

It was hard work. He learned new things about himself and was asked to delve into the past so that he could find healing. Alcoholism was the symptom, but there was deeper work that needed to be done.

Maybe you believe this story has nothing to do with you, but the common theme—whether it's my loved one, Peter the apostle, or you or me—is this:

We don't know what we don't know, but that doesn't mean we are stuck.

The Counselor meets us right where we are. We may feel a little lost, but he shows us which way to turn. We may not see around the corner, but we can trust that he does. We understand there is a learning curve, but we are willing to become students. We know that God has a plan—for the church, for our loved ones, and for us—so we show up, listen, and follow where he leads.

If God is the one speaking, his voice must be louder than any other in our ear.

Louder than what a person says.

Louder than our reservations.

Louder than our fears.

Louder than a cultural belief or prejudice.

In every part of this relationship, the Counselor remains near. He knows our thoughts, but it's God's thoughts that he conveys. He's watching to see if we stay on the path, and he speaks when we start to stray.

We may not see God. We may feel that we are over our head. We may wonder if we'll ever get there. Like that three-year-old who felt he was lost, we hear these words:

If you think you are lost, just stop.

I know right where to find you.

I know the plans the Father has for you.

Listen for my voice. I'm here. I'll show you the way.

The Word

As for you, the anointing you received from him remains in you, and you do not need anyone to teach you. But as his anointing teaches you about all things and as that anointing is real, not counterfeit—just as it has taught you, remain in him.

1 JOHN 2:27

Your Spirit-Led Promise

You will never be without counsel.

Your Spirit-Led Invitation

Discover what you don't know and be changed.

Prayer

Open my ears to hear. I'm willing to be changed, challenged, and counseled, for God reveals these things through you. If there are things that I'm allowing to shut out your voice, show me. I'll give them their proper place in my life. Thank you for bringing the Word to life, so that I might live my faith more fully.

8

We Recognize What Is Unseen

A Spirit-Led Heart Finds
Discernment and Wisdom

Discernment is not a matter of simply telling the difference between right and wrong; rather it is telling the difference between right and almost right.

Charles Spurgeon

Granny lived in rural Arkansas. I was a city girl. When we pulled up in our white Buick with my parents and siblings, I slipped my flip-flops on. The grass was filled with prickly burrs that liked to work their way into the tender underside of my feet.

Granny lived in a small white house off a long dirt road.

A propane tank fueled the kitchen stove, where she made chocolate pies. The water was ice cold but turned sandy brown if you let it run too long. Granny's home was as different as could be from the city streets and crowded neighborhood where we lived. When we visited, I loved to walk in the nearby protected forest, picking up crystal rocks and shining them on my shirt. There weren't many places off limits.

Except for the whale.

Granny pointed to an area of the yard when I was young. It was a small boarded-over area at the right front of the house. "Stay away from that," she said. "That's the whale."

I was fascinated by the fact that my granny had a whale in her front yard. I imagined an underground spring so large that it held the great fish. The area was rife with springs, and it wasn't unusual to see water bubbling up out of the ground in surprising places.

I did exactly what Granny told me to do. I stayed away from the whale. I'd walk twenty feet out of the way to avoid it, imagining what would happen if the faded plywood were to crumble under my thin frame and I fell into the whale's home.

We visited Granny's only once or twice a year as I got older. At the age of twelve, I went to visit Granny with the family. I walked over to the forbidden area and heard Granny's words clearly for the first time.

"Stay away from the whale."

Except she wasn't saying "whale" at all.

Her accent was typical for that part of the state, and it held a delightful twang.

"Suzie, stay away from the well."

The well was covered, but if I were to pull back the boards out of curiosity, it could be dangerous. The well was deep. Thus, the warning.

I laughed out loud at myself for holding that vision of a whale for so many years.

It seems silly now, but the image of a whale slipped into the imagination of a little girl and stayed there for way too long. I don't know why I didn't figure it out sooner, but the truth is that because I stayed away from that area, I didn't give it a lot of thought.

I didn't tell a soul about that story for years.

I feel a little sheepish telling you now.

The Early Church: Seeing beyond the Obvious

Discernment is an attribute of the Holy Spirit. He unmasks false teaching, reveals misleading doctrines, and unveils deceptive tactics used by the enemy to distract or harm the body of Christ. The early church met these types of distractions often.

When we drop in to the early church in Acts 12–15, the church is thriving in many ways, but it's also just as beleaguered as ever. Peter is in jail again. He's considered such a spiritual threat that there are four squads of four soldiers guarding him. He's shackled with chains.

Meanwhile, the church has gathered to pray. They are at the home of Mary, the mother of John Mark, fasting and interceding for Peter. Their prayers reach heaven and then drop into a dirty jail cell. Peter hears a clank, and then another as his chains drop. He is free, though there are guards at two posts between him and the massive iron gate.

Led by an angel, Peter makes it past all of them. It is as if the guards are blind and deaf. As he approaches the gate, it opens on its own. A miracle! Peter runs to Mary's home and bangs on the door. A servant girl named Rhoda opens the door and is so stunned by the disheveled apostle that she slams the door in his face. Peter continues to bang on the door until his friends come and open it in amazement.

What a powerful scene!

Peter goes back to leading the church. Paul and Barnabas take off for Pathos, where they meet a sorcerer. He has labeled himself a prophet and attached himself to the governor. This false prophet is intimidated by Paul's genuine faith, so he distorts the truth to the governor.

Paul, filled with the Holy Spirit, looks the sorcerer in the eye. "Will you never stop perverting the true ways of the Lord?"

Suddenly, the sorcerer loses his sight. The governor witnesses all of this and is convinced that Paul's version of faith is the truth (Acts 13:9–12).

Later Paul travels to Antioch to visit a new church community. The problem is that some men have infiltrated the church and are teaching that every new convert must be circumcised or their faith isn't genuine. By demanding that new believers be circumcised, they are tying them to the old law—the law that Jesus fulfilled, the old covenant that Jesus said had passed away. Paul loves these fledgling churches and the people that fill them. He grieves that their newfound faith has been confused by well-meaning people or false prophets.

I've been a believer for four decades. I can point to confusing doctrine that has placed a burden on new believers, or well-meaning teaching spoken with great authority but lacking mercy. In every instance, it was vital to know the difference between what was true and what was *almost* true.

Discernment helps us tell the difference between what is true and what is almost true.

When Peter's shackles fall off, it takes faith to walk past the guards and through a maze of protective walls and gates. Peter has to trust what he cannot see in the natural, as he is led by the supernatural. It feels right, but what about the guards? What about the locked gate that stands higher than any man can scale? Holy Spirit discernment is his green light, his caution, and his stop sign, if needed.

When Paul meets the sorcerer, it is a little more obvious. The sorcerer is a false prophet who is distorting truth. Paul doesn't need discernment to know that the guy is a fraud. He does, however, need discernment to know how to deal with this man. When Paul rebukes the false prophet, he also rebukes the one behind the lies.

In Antioch, it's much more complex.

The guys who insist on circumcision aren't bad people. They are Pharisees who have converted to Christianity. Their intent isn't evil, but their doctrine is misleading. It has the potential to harm the church and place a burden back on believers that Jesus removed. Paul and Barnabas reemphasize the promise of the cross and Jesus's resurrection. They remind believers of the freedom they have received.

> "God knows people's hearts, and he confirmed that he accepts Gentiles *by giving them the Holy Spirit*, just as he did to us. He made no distinction between us and them, for he cleansed their hearts through faith."
>
> Acts 15:8–9 NLT

They don't get angry at the Pharisees, but they speak truth into the matter.

Discernment searches the truth. It knows the truth. It lives the truth.

When we are unsure of what's going on, we don't lead in with our own understanding. Whether in leadership or ministry or the cloud of confusion over a relationship, family, or job, we can ask the Holy Spirit to show us what we cannot see in the natural.

The early church dealt with confusion. We will too.

The Holy Spirit helps us to differentiate between right and *almost* right.

He shows us what to do about it.

Your Promise: You Will See Behind the Curtain

In the classic movie *The Wizard of Oz,* the wizard is no wizard at all. He's a hustler from Kansas, and he's been conning the people of Oz for years. When Toto pulls back the curtain, the wizard tries to keep up the disguise, but it's too late. Dorothy and her crew are on to his scheme.

Holy Spirit discernment pulls back the curtain.

Recently, my husband and I were picking up a few items at a store. A man approached us. I thought he looked slightly familiar, and so did his wife, who stood nearby.

"Did you hear what I heard?" he asked.

I had no idea what he was talking about.

He went on to share his dissatisfaction with a message he had heard in church. Evidently, we had been visiting the same church at the same time, which is why he stopped us.

I recalled the message he was talking about. I knew the person who taught it well. While I didn't get to hear this person teach often, when I did, it was challenging and uplifting. It was clear that he studied and taught the Word with depth and practical application. The man in the store continued to share that he thought the message was "shocking," which led to other things he thought the pastor had said or done in error.

I didn't know what to do.

Two minutes earlier I was loading my grocery cart with V8 juice, and now I was listening to something my spirit was telling me was wrong. Not only was it off-kilter, it was damaging. There's nothing more discouraging than faithfully serving in any capacity, only to be picked apart. If I continued to listen, I was complicit.

All I wanted was to pick up a few groceries. This man thought he was correcting a wrong, but that doesn't mean he was right—in either his assumptions or his approach.

Richard had stood quietly beside me, taking it all in.

"I think he's a really great teacher," he said. He wasn't confrontational, because my guy never is. His words were soft and measured.

"Well, he's not much of a teacher if he said . . ."

It was clear that we weren't going to be able to persuade him.

I told the man gently that I was also a Bible teacher. I said that if someone disagreed with something I taught, I'd welcome them to come to me. I'd much rather hear from them directly than for that person to be upset privately. "Maybe you could talk with him about your reservations," I said as gently as I could.

The man was affronted.

We finally loaded up our tomato juice and said our good-byes. We couldn't change this man's mind, but we didn't have to listen to him tear down a good man who worked hard to love people.

You and I aren't likely to meet a sorcerer on the street.

We probably aren't going to be chained in jail and hear our shackles fall to the ground.

We will, however, be a part of a ministry or community that has disagreements. We will be the recipient of someone's hurtful words, whether there is ill motive or not. We will meet people with agendas that aren't scriptural and who have the power to do a lot of harm. Sometimes we'll think we are in the right, but we handle it all wrong. It's in these moments that we need discernment. We need the Holy Spirit to peel back the curtain to see beyond the obvious.

We need to pay attention when our spirit is in turmoil.

I try to believe the best before assuming the worst. In this case, I believe this man's motivation was to protect the Word. The way he was handling his dissatisfaction was far from helpful, however. While he spoke, my spirit was in turmoil.

> And do not bring sorrow to God's Holy Spirit by the way you live.
>
> Ephesians 4:30 NLT

The Holy Spirit can be grieved, and that's what I sensed. He was grieved by the interaction. There was much to be grieved in that pick-apart conversation taking place. And if I stayed there any longer, I would also grieve him.

> Get rid of all bitterness, rage, anger, harsh words, and slander, as well as all types of evil behavior. Instead, be kind to each other, tenderhearted, forgiving one another, just as God through Christ has forgiven you.
>
> Ephesians 4:31–32 NLT

The conversation wasn't living up to Scripture. I prayed silently, because I wasn't sure how to handle the situation. As certain as I was that the man was approaching this in the wrong way, I know I am capable of doing the same.

When we are uncertain, our tendency is to stay stuck in the conversation or in the place we aren't supposed to be. We worry about hurting someone's feelings if we don't listen. We don't want to make waves or create controversy. We wrestle with how to do what the Holy Spirit is clearly speaking to us, but there's no graceful way out.

When my children were teens, we had a house rule: If you ever find yourself in a place you shouldn't be—even if you were the one who took yourself there—call. Let us know that you aren't where you are supposed to be, and we'll come get you. We'll honor the fact that you were smart enough to make a different and wiser choice.

In some ways, discernment gives us that same grace.

First John 4:1 tells us to "test the spirits." If they aren't from God, make that call.

> *Lord, I'm unsure what I'm supposed to do. All I know is that I'm here, and it's not where you want me to be. Give me wisdom to know your will for me right now. Give me courage to step away from this conversation, or to speak up if that is what you want. Don't allow fear or anxiousness to keep me stuck in something that grieves the Holy Spirit.*

Richard and I were given a glimpse beyond the obvious. It's why we prayed in the car afterward. We prayed for clarity for this couple. We prayed protection over this pastor and his family, who had to deal with these hurtful conversations. We prayed that we handled it correctly and, if not, to know what to do about that.

Your Invitation: Take Spiritual Authority over the Enemy

The Holy Spirit unmasks false teaching, reveals misleading doctrines, and unveils deceptive tactics used by the enemy to distract or harm the body of Christ. We've discussed false teaching and misleading doctrine, but we can't walk with the early church and dismiss the fact that the apostles encountered people who were tormented (Acts 8:7; 16:18; 19:12–13).

Throughout Scripture, Jesus came across men and women who were desperate, whether due to sickness, mental illness, or oppression. He addressed the source of pain while validating the person in front of him with empathy and kindness. It's one of the most powerful characteristics of our faith and about our Savior.

In my ministry travels around the world, I've met women who struggle in ways I cannot comprehend. As I've prayed with them, I've had glimpses into their burdens. The Holy Spirit has gently pulled back the curtain. In those moments, all I know to do is to pray in the name of Jesus. To tell the woman in front of me that she is loved by her heavenly Father and that Jesus came to rescue her. I pray the Holy Spirit would reveal truth to her—that she is loved, she is seen, she is not alone.

I can't tell you exactly what the battle is, but it's something she didn't ask for and longs to be free of. When we talk afterward, the woman is often embarrassed by her pain. But she also feels hope that she too can be free. Just knowing that God doesn't shy away from her torment is pivotal.

When we encounter those who are tormented or oppressed, our response can be unhealthy. We might glorify the enemy by walking in fear, or dismiss the enemy and blame the troubled person.

There's a third option, and it's where Jesus walked. It's a mix of spiritual discernment and mercy.

I remember one moment with a woman, not because of a startling scene but because God peeled away the curtain to show the battle and his heart for her. By doing so, he allowed me to respond in a way that loosed the enemy's hold—and a troubled woman realized that Jesus saw her, loved her, and was reaching for her.

Holy Spirit Discernment without Borders

It's not our job to ferret out misleading doctrine, false teaching, or oppression. We aren't spiritual ghostbusters. We'll encounter these dangers without seeking them out.

Holy Spirit discernment hones in on the real battle. Usually that fight is best fought on our knees in prayer, but there will be other times when we need the right word or an exit strategy, or perhaps wisdom to address the underlying issue.

Discernment is closely tied to wisdom. When you wait for that spiritual insight, long before acting or reacting, it's wise. You are able to deal with that person or situation entirely differently. When you are unsure of how to respond, it's vital to pay attention to the Holy Spirit who lives in you. Long before you say anything. Long before you talk to another person about it. Long before those feelings get in the way. Waiting allows you to respond with grace, or in some cases, with spiritual wisdom and authority.

As you listen for Holy Spirit discernment, honor that feeling that says, "This could hurt my church," "This isn't your job," or "Their motivations aren't pure." Discernment is also key in your own decisions. If you are hurt or angry, ask the Holy Spirit to help you distinguish what is going on beneath the surface. If you feel that twinge that asks, "Are you doing this for the right reason?" pay attention.

These are discerning questions to ask in almost every uncertain situation:

- Holy Spirit, is there something here that I'm not seeing?
- What is a God-honoring way to respond?
- Will you give me wisdom and insight that I need in this moment?

It's never too late to slow a situation down. You may have been warring for months with a feeling or a person or a situation. Stop long enough to ask these questions. The answers might not come immediately, but when you ask, it creates spiritual room so that answers can come.

Holy Spirit discernment separates true from *almost* true. We don't have to spend our lives believing a giant whale will get us when it's only a tiny well in the ground. For too many years I feared the wrong thing. Discernment identifies the real danger and shows how to deal with it.

We'll have multiple opportunities to use discernment, and the result is a wise heart, not easily distracted or led astray.

The Word

Dear friends, do not believe everyone who claims to speak by the Spirit. You must test them to see if the spirit they have comes from God. For there are many false prophets in the world.

1 JOHN 4:1 NLT

Your Spirit-Led Promise

He'll show you the difference
between truth and *almost* truth.

Your Spirit-Led Invitation

See behind the curtain.

Prayer

I need a Spirit-led discerning heart. Before I rush in or make judgment, help me to see beyond the immediate. Thank you for protecting me. Thank you for pulling back the veil so that I can see more clearly. In Jesus's name, amen.

9

We Love Our Faith, but We *Live* Our Faith

A Spirit-Led Heart Is Marked by Conviction

> Having convictions is being so thoroughly convinced
> that Christ and his Word are both objectively true and
> relationally meaningful that you act on your beliefs
> regardless of the consequences.
>
> Josh McDowell, *Beyond Belief to Convictions*

The couple owned a gorgeous house. It had two stories and was huge compared to the house they had when their children were growing up. Every detail was planned in advance. They loved their home! They opened it to friends and hosted small groups for new members in their church.

They believed every inch of that home belonged to God.

One day they felt they were supposed to put it on the market. It's not what they thought they'd do when they so painstakingly built it. It wasn't an easy decision, but they had a reason. If they sold their dream home, they could buy a smaller home with a smaller mortgage. They desired to give more to ministries they believed were impacting lives.

The home sold quickly.

They packed up their belongings, said good-bye to their dream home, and drove the moving truck to the smaller older house several blocks away.

When I heard their story, I asked them to share more about their decision. They were almost embarrassed to tell their story. They didn't see this as a sacrifice, but as a natural part of living their faith. If God was leading them to do anything, they wanted to obey. Selling their home was an outward, but private, mark of their beliefs. They didn't tell anyone except their children at first why they sold it. When they moved their furniture into the smaller home with lots of projects waiting to be done, they didn't dwell on it.

Selling their dream home allowed them to give in greater measure. That was their focus.

They showed me a picture of the home they had sold. I saw loving details that the man, a craftsman, had put into the house.

"Do you miss it?" I asked.

"Sure," they both replied, but added almost in unison, "but we are exactly where we are supposed to be."

Reading this might make your heart beat a little faster.

Is God asking me to sell my house?

That's not the point of this story. It's that this couple live their faith. It is more than a feeling, more than being a member of a church. It is a walk of obedience and joy and hard choices.

The early church didn't just love their faith, they lived it. There was an element of sacrifice in almost everything they did. As they followed Jesus, they took up their cross daily (Matthew 16:24).

Their faith was linked to their convictions. They could tell you why they believed the way they did. They often shared those beliefs with close friends and family, but for the most part they lived the sermon.

A lot of us love our faith.

I do. It's such a gift! I love grace. I embrace mercy. I adore God's love and being called his daughter. I am grateful for comfort that comes from above. I am thankful for provision for my basic needs and for those of my loved ones. I delight that I pray and God hears me.

All of these are integral parts of our faith, but there's more.

We love our faith, but conviction changes how we *live* our faith. We believe to the point that it affects our choices. It filters our words. It's instrumental in those moments when no one is looking. It redefines what we consider important or lasting and what we invest ourselves and our resources in. It affects the way we view material goods—not as bad or good, but as belonging to God. We understand faith is often sacrificial, but with the understanding that the greatest sacrifice has already been made on our behalf.

I haven't been asked to sell my home, but I have been asked to let go of unforgiveness, or to believe in the impossible. I've been asked to see myself the way he does. I've learned to hold everything I own or love loosely.

For years I limited faith to being loved by God, because I was still maturing in my faith. Like a child, I saw only my needs and God as my need-meeter. I couldn't help but be grateful for that love. As I matured, I realized that, while God loved me, he wanted me to love him back.

If I say I love something, but I'm not willing to give myself to it, it's still in the flirting stage.

Deep, committed love is sacrificial. It takes time to build. There may be times we are angry at God, but we work through it. We talk to him. The longer we know him, the more we start to look like him (Colossians 3:10).

God isn't interested in how much we own, what we pile up, or how high up the ladder we climb; but he absolutely asks us to use those things to love others in his name.

What is conviction? It's knowing what we believe.

We know whom we love and why. We are disciples, not just hearers of the Word. We believe that the Word can take root in us and that it can change a world.

Conviction will always take us into deeper waters of faith.

Believing is falling, getting back up, growing through our mistakes, reaching for mercy, communing with God, and running after his heart. Holy Spirit conviction helps us to live our faith one day at a time until it becomes the core of our spiritual (and earthly) identity.

The Early Church: The Church Matures

In the remaining chapters in the book of Acts, the original disciples—Peter, Thomas, Bartholomew, John, Andrew, and others—seem to fade away in the story. The book of Acts spans a period of years.

We get glimpses of these men throughout other books in the Bible. These glimpses, along with historical accounts, help fill in the blanks.

Their faith never fades. Most will be martyred. Others will keep busy doing the work of the church. Persecution sends the apostles and followers of Christ across several different countries. The apostles will age but are on the go until the end.

None of them will lose their love for Jesus or for the gospel.

New names emerge in the book of Acts. We have already become familiar with Paul and Barnabas, but now we read about young Timothy, John Mark, Silas, Lydia, Priscilla and Aquila, Justus, and many others who play a role in the church.

Luke, the Gentile physician, is the author of the book of Acts. If we were sitting across from him, we might ask him why he didn't carry the story of the original apostles all the way through the book of Acts. We might ask why he left the story of Paul dangling in the last chapter. It's not a very satisfying conclusion! Luke leaves Paul in Rome, though there's a lot more of his story to tell. He will eventually lose his life for his faith.

Some describe life as the dash between the years—the time between the year of birth and the year of death. Paul lives his dash well. He writes letter after letter to churches. He preaches and lives a beautiful sermon until the moment he loses his life for his faith and crosses the threshold from earth to eternity.

The book of Acts is not about any one person but about the church. There's only one name that shows up from first chapter to the last, and that's the Holy Spirit.

We get to witness how this gift of a Helper worked in the church. We get to see a church empowered and launched, fueled and watched over by the Holy Spirit. We see a pattern that develops in the story of the early church.

They believe.

They are called.

They preach and teach. They pray.

Some believe. Others don't. Some love them. Others hate them. Some don't care.

They are welcomed. They are rejected. They are mocked. They are questioned. They are beaten. They are imprisoned.

There are miracles, spiritual and physical.

They are filled and refilled with the Holy Spirit.

Their convictions lead them wherever God wants them to be.

They believe.

Once again, it's the dash. These people are spiritually birthed, and even in death they live. They believe so firmly that martyrdom is welcomed. Unlike martyrdom that is willing to damage and kill others for a false reward, they sacrificially live their faith to love others until the very end.

Because Jesus loved them first.

Our faith journey begins and ends with belief.

There are a lot of ups and downs in between. If we didn't have belief or conviction, Acts 16 through 28 would leave us feeling yanked about as if by a giant bungee cord. The early church feels the ups and downs. They are forced to respond to them. They live the dash fully—strong and steady—because they believe faith in an almighty God is a gift of great measure.

Conviction is the belief that what you are doing is real and has substance. It's the belief that faith truly does change you and others. You know that God sent Jesus to save the world, and he reached for you in the process. You are convinced of the power of prayer. You believe you are called to follow Jesus in every part of your life. There's nothing held back from him. He has a say in what you do and who you are, and you embrace it.

Those fishermen, farmers, and tax collectors believed, and their convictions were so strong that they left a mark on the world. It caused others to take a second listen, and they believed too. That imprint is still creating miracles in the hearts of people today.

Do we really understand the power of belief?

Do we?

Lord, help me to live my faith, not just love it. That feels like a dangerous prayer, but I'm praying it anyway. Thank you for the sweetness of faith, but I also embrace the cross. Father, let my children, my neighbors, the guy who checks out my groceries see you in me. Let my private life match my public faith, but go even deeper because that's where I meet you. Lord, let my convictions and belief in you speak gently to those seeking, those hungry for truth, and those who have lost their way.

Your Promise: Your Faith Has Substance

We identify ourselves as believers in a lot of ways. Like T-shirts. I love the ones with super soft fabric and cool fonts.

There are wall plaques and bumper stickers. We put snazzy sayings on social media like "Grace-girl who loves a perfect cup of coffee but is thankful that God loves my imperfect heart." We are identified as we read the Bible on a park bench while the kids play, or by the fact that we support and attend a local church.

All good things.

Yet belief and conviction aren't always soft and comfortable. I've had to choose to say no to things that others find harmless—things you might find a little ridiculous. I'm not listing them because what's off-limits for me may not be off-limits for you. There are times the Holy Spirit says no to me about something, but it would be perfectly okay for you—and vice versa.

We have guidelines in Scripture that show us what to do or not to do. Yet some areas not so concrete, because Scripture addresses the condition of our hearts. That's where we can get a little lost. We try to live by a list of what to do or what not do, try to figure out what is acceptable. And we're confused when it's not clear-cut.

Belief isn't a list of what we say yes or no to; it's believing that our God is worthy of a life of surrender.

> And now you Gentiles have also heard the truth, the Good News that God saves you. And when you believed in Christ, *he identified you as his own by giving you the Holy Spirit*, whom he promised long ago.
>
> Ephesians 1:13 NLT

When we live our faith, we become marked. We are identified by the Holy Spirit as believers. We become vehicles of faith as the Holy Spirit shows us how to live so that others will want Jesus too.

In the past few years, I've been privileged to walk with extraordinary but ordinary people who not only love their faith but absolutely live it.

Like the couple who sold their home so they could give more generously. Or the family that adopted a severely disabled child, and then started an organization from scratch for other parents with severely disabled children. There's the owner of a small boutique that sells donated upscale clothing and jewelry. The prices are fabulous, but what I love most is that the owner donates the profits to four local and global ministries.

They are kingdom builders.

I met a family who started an after-school program for underserved children seventeen years ago. That ministry branched out beyond their imagination. They now employ a large team and host camps, and many of their staff and volunteers, including the founders, have opened their homes to children who are in crisis. They expanded the ministry to include teens (because the little ones grew up!) and are continually brainstorming ways to love this growing community with integrity and dignity.

It's not easy work, but it's become their life.

Another family bought a small cottage in an isolated scenic area. Their plan is that Mom and Dad will enjoy it one day in their retirement years. For now, it's a private getaway when they need alone time. It's not a resort area. It's not fancy. It's a one-bedroom, one-bath cottage nestled in the Ozarks. They don't get to spend as much time there as they want because they are still working and engaged with family and ministry. In the meantime, they share it freely with pastors, missionaries, and others in full-time ministry at no cost.

When I found out within the space of a few days that both my daughter and mother had cancer, I was in the end stretch of studying for and writing this book. The owner of the cottage sent a message to me and invited me to use it as a sanctuary to finish the book. It was an answer to prayer. I drove an hour to the small cottage and hung out with their border collie, Winnie, for four days. The Lord and I spent hours together. I presented my hurting mama-daughter heart to him and unloaded my burden. I lit candles, ate Peanut M&M's, and watched the sun set over the beautiful Ozark mountains as I wrote.

The most amazing thing about her invitation is that we had never met.

She reached out because the Lord had placed me on her heart. She had no idea what was going on in my personal life. That simple gesture helped put my upside-down emotions back on axis. It helped me write this book.

None of the people I mentioned are in the Forbes Top 100.

None of them have had a photo on the cover of a national magazine.

For the most part, they are behind the scenes. Their sacrificial choices are unnoticed because they don't do them for people. There are no press releases or social media announcements. They do what they do because their convictions are anchored in their belief in God.

They may have T-shirts that tell about their faith, but it's their lives that are the story.

> But when the kindness and love of God our Savior appeared, he saved us, not because of righteous things we had done, but because of his mercy. He saved us through the washing *of rebirth and renewal by the Holy Spirit*, whom he poured out on us generously through Jesus Christ our Savior, so that, having been justified by his grace, we might become heirs having the hope of eternal life.
>
> Titus 3:4–7

We are not saved by what we do. That leads to striving.

We live our faith because of what he's already done for us. We aren't looking for anything in return.

Our faith is renewed by the Holy Spirit, which impacts the way we live, and this creates a ripple effect. If the early church had been dependent on being good or moral alone, they might as well have remained under the old covenant law. The Holy Spirit took the church's eyes off what they were doing and focused them on whom they loved. They were identified or stamped as believers.

The Holy Spirit invites us to become a vehicle for his spirit. We love our faith, but we are empowered to live our faith with conviction.

What does that look like?

> Having convictions is being so thoroughly convinced that Christ and His Word are both objectively true and relationally meaningful that you act on your beliefs regardless of the consequences.[1]

A Spirit-led heart is convicted when we fall short, but our convictions lead us to ask for help, forgiveness, and restoration. A Spirit-led heart isn't satisfied with a spoonful of faith here or there, for Holy Spirit conviction kindles our desire to know him.

Conviction believes there is joy in following Jesus.

Conviction says that we will do what he asks simply because he is the one asking.

A Spirit-led heart is open to all that God has for us, even if that comes in the wilderness. A Spirit-led heart is never a know-it-all, but desires to know it all—the depths of what faith offers.

Your Invitation: Establish Your Core Beliefs

What if you were asked to stand in front of a crowd and say what you believe? I can hear the knees knocking from here!

At every challenge from authority, Peter, John, or Paul preached a sermon. Really long sermons too. They reached back to the prophets and carried the message all the way to Jesus. They weren't afraid to tell people that they were once a mess, and how Jesus saved them. They were quick to dismiss anything other than Christ that might label them as good or worthy.

> Then Paul said: "I am a Jew, born in Tarsus of Cilicia, but brought up in this city. I studied under Gamaliel and was thoroughly trained in the law of our ancestors. I was just as zealous for God as any of you are today. I persecuted the followers of this Way to their death, arresting both men and women and throwing them into prison, as the high priest and all the Council can themselves testify."
>
> Acts 22:2–5

Thousands of people were converted because of their words, but also because of their example. People couldn't help but notice that even when they were thrown in prison, they didn't quit talking about Jesus. That when they spoke about Jesus, it was as if they were speaking of a friend—who was also the Messiah.

People weren't converted because the apostles' messages were wise, witty, and entertaining. They were swayed because the apostles' faith influenced every part of their being.

When we base our identity as Christians on a system, a set of rules, a cultural label, it gets murky—because those things aren't God. Our faith influences those things, but it is not replaced by them. Our invitation is to be marked by faith alone.

Conviction without Borders

The sun was lowering, and the hazy orange skyline was beautiful.

"Suzie, why do you call yourself a Christian?"

I didn't see the question coming. We were with friends of friends—I'll call them Jack and Emily—who had come to town and needed a place to stay. We had an open room. Both families had come for dinner. We had a big meal, played some cards, and then sat out on the deck and listened to music.

It was perfect.

Now everyone but Jack and I had gone inside. Emily was putting their girls down for the night. I sat quietly enjoying the sunset. He leaned against the stairway, waiting for his wife to rejoin him.

"Why do you call yourself a Christian?"

"What?" I asked, wondering if I had heard his question correctly.

I knew a little about his story. He had grown up in a Christian home but decided as an adult it wasn't for him. I wasn't sure how to answer his question. All the Scriptures—like the Romans Road to Salvation—came tumbling in my brain, but that's not usually how I share my faith. I wasn't supposed to pull out a Paul-like sermon that reached from the prophets to the cross.

"I can't imagine my life without my faith," I answered.

"What do you mean?"

"It's who I am. I'm loved by God, and I feel that every day. I can't imagine my life without such a gift."

He nodded. "Okay."

I beat myself up for that answer later. I didn't share even one Scripture. I didn't tell him what God had done for me. I wondered if I had missed a God-moment.

Good grief, I'm a communicator, and I was far from eloquent!

The next day they climbed into their car and drove home. They were strangers, really, and it wasn't likely we'd cross paths again.

Almost a year later, I ran into our mutual friends. "What did you say to him?" the woman asked.

"Who?"

"What did you say to Jack when they visited?"

My answer to his question seemed so insufficient at the time that I was certain she was referring to something else. "I'm not sure what you are talking about."

"Our friends who stayed at your home. He said you showed him Jesus in a way that he hadn't thought about. He's been really open to faith since then. He's reading books about faith, and I won't be surprised if he becomes a believer soon."

I was stunned. To this day, I realize how inadequate my words were. But I meant them. Every single word.

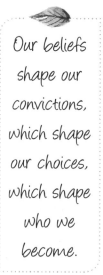

Our beliefs shape our convictions, which shape our choices, which shape who we become.

I can't imagine my life without faith in Christ.

I can't imagine a life without the love of my heavenly Father.

I love that the Holy Spirit can take heartfelt words and plant them like seeds in rugged soil. This man grew up in church. He knew all of the reasons he *should* believe.

He was asking why I believed.

A Spirit-led heart knows what she believes. It's who she is and what she is becoming. She's convinced that God loves her, and moreover, she loves him back. That belief shapes her convictions, which shape her choices, which shape who she becomes.

Conviction leads us toward belief, but also away from sin. It takes the shiny paint off of sin. Why in the world would we want something that is of such lesser value than our faith?

A woman once asked me if I was tempted when I traveled. She wondered if I ever flirted or liked flirting. I'm not sure why she asked. I told her that no one is above temptation, but that something rises within me if a person crosses that line.

That something that rises asks, *Do you think you are more valuable than the man I've loved for nearly four decades? Do you think you are worth destroying the way my children look at me, or worth hurting the hearts of the six littles who believe I'm a safe place for them?*

Belief and conviction are absolutely part of this, but the foundation is that I love what I've been given. It's such a gift. There's nothing worth harming that for. The temptation to flirt or be flirted with isn't flattering at all, because it has the power to rob me of something precious.

Yet I'm tempted in other areas. I'm tempted to be discouraged when I work really hard and there's not a lot of success to show for it. I'm tempted to be angry when someone hurts my feelings. I'm tempted to give up when I hit a wall of resistance or when there are difficult people involved.

We will never be above temptation, but when we love the Lord, we do count the cost.

> The Spirit-filled life is not a special, deluxe edition of Christianity. It is part and parcel of the total plan of God for His people.
>
> A. W. Tozer[2]

Belief leads us—sometimes to deep waters where we have to trust God utterly. To sacrificial choices that don't make sense to anyone else, but make perfect sense to you because you've prayed and wrestled with them.

It leads you to believe in something or in someone when it's not culturally popular.

You seek truth, because truth matters to God.

And yes, you remain that woman who loves a perfect cup of coffee (or a steaming cup of hot chocolate), and who is thankful that God loves your imperfect heart.

The Word

May the God of hope fill you with all joy and peace in believing, so that by the power of the Holy Spirit you may abound in hope.

ROMANS 15:13 ESV

Your Spirit-Led Promise

Your beliefs become convictions,
which shape who you become.

Your Spirit-Led Invitation

Love your faith, but also live it.

Prayer

Scrape away anything that isn't faith in you. I give you all that I am, all that I own, all that I love. You love me, and I'm forever thankful. Let my life reflect that I love you back. You aren't asking me to be something I'm not, but to follow you with all that I am. What a privilege!

10

Good Gifts Make Us Stronger

A Spirit-Led Heart Is
Gifted

I have prayed for help and for the influences of the Holy Spirit, but I always thought that they were to be given to me and then I was to resist my own enemies and fight my own battles. And consequently I depended upon my own efforts, my own resolutions, my own watchfulness, my own fervency, my own strivings to accomplish the work of holy living.

Hannah Whitall Smith

Ding-ding-ding. Ding-ding-diiiiing.

Whoever was in control of the doorbell wasn't going to let up until I answered. It was Christmas. Smells of turkey, dressing, and sweet potatoes with fluffy marshmallows permeated the room. When I opened the door, one of my six littles tumbled in and threw her arms around my legs. Another child pushed by her and grabbed my other leg.

The less assertive littles were behind, and one by one they ran in.

All were aware that there were presents under the tree—the gifts had been there for a few days. They were kids, so presents were a big deal. While they waited to unwrap gifts, they clambered to be on my lap. One sat near, telling me about his day so far. Another wrapped his arms around my neck, telling me in my ear that he had missed me. They were excited for Christmas to begin, but they were also excited to be with me.

There are a lot of sweet (and chaotic) memories from that Christmas, but that memory is the sweetest.

Let's consider another scene.

Ding-ding-ding. Ding-ding-diiiiing.

The house is sweet with the anointed presence of God. An abundance of gifts wait to be opened. They have been specially chosen, and each has a distinct purpose. The door is opened, and God's children run past without even a hello. They plunge into the gifts and start unwrapping them. They try them out, tossing some to the side and holding others in a tight grip. A fight erupts over which gift is for whom and which is the most valuable.

The door still stands open.

Did they notice the One who stood at the door, or were they only interested in his gifts?

Why are they fighting over gifts when there are enough to go around?

What about those gifts tossed to the side? Do they not know that those gifts are of great worth too?

You may wonder why I left the gifts of the Holy Spirit until the last chapter. It's not because they are not important, but my desire in writing *The Spirit-Led Heart* was to spend time with the Helper, long before we unwrap the gifts given to help build the church.

The Early Church: The Gifts Make Them Stronger

The acts of the early church produce actual churches—the church of Corinth, the church of Ephesus, the Thessalonian church, and many others. Some are launched by the apostles. Some are built by believers whose names we don't know. They simply share their faith, and people are influenced to follow Christ.

> Some of them, however, men from Cyprus and Cyrene, went to Antioch and began to speak to Greeks also, telling them the good news about the Lord Jesus. The Lord's hand was with them, and a great number of people believed and turned to the Lord.
>
> Acts 11:20–21

In Acts 18, Paul is mentoring one of the new churches, the church of Corinth. He's a church planter but also a spiritual father. He has been with this church for a year and a half, and that's unusual for him. He usually plants a church and then moves to the next.

It hasn't been an easy eighteen months. Corinth has a bad reputation as a trade city bustling with evil and sexual sin. Prostitution is woven through pagan and idol worship.

Some Corinthians have been receptive and even eager for Paul's message. Others fight him like crazy. Paul remains, in spite of how hard it is, because these believers are babes in the faith. They are working through twisted religious thinking to find truth. They are also arguing with each other, so much so that Paul is really discouraged. But the Lord encourages him to keep going (Acts 18:9).

If God is in it, then he'll provide what is needed to stay strong.

Paul writes a letter to this church. That letter becomes what we know as 1 Corinthians. In it, he teaches what is faith and what is not. He speaks about the spiritual gifts. Paul writes this letter because the church of Corinth is acting a little like unruly children at an out-of-control birthday party. The spiritual gifts are in operation within the church, but some are seen as more desired while others are underappreciated. Some believers boast about their gifting, while others are dismayed because they want that same gift.

The word *gift* makes us think of a bow-tied present. Yet this word isn't an accurate representation. If we take it deeper to reflect what Paul is saying, we discover it means these spiritual gifts are valuable because of who gives them.

> There are different kinds of gifts, but the same Spirit distributes them. There are different kinds of service, but the same Lord. . . . Now to each one the manifestation of the Spirit is given for the common good.
>
> 1 Corinthians 12:4–7

I have a few precious things. They wouldn't qualify as treasures to some, but they are to me because of the story behind them.

I found a smooth hammer-shaped rock buried in the ground in the woods of an Oklahoma forest. I was five years old. I loved it because it was unusual. It had grainy symmetrical lines. Later I discovered it was a genuine Native American tomahawk. I took that treasure to show-and-tell when I was in elementary school, and today my grandchildren love to hold it and hear the story of how I found it.

The spiritual gifts aren't prized because they make us special, or even because they are powerful standing on their own. They are valuable because the Giver gave them so that we could help each other.

Paul doesn't want the church to be ignorant of these spiritual gifts (1 Corinthians 12:1). When I was a little girl, I thought that the word *ignorant* meant "stupid." It doesn't mean that at all, not in the true sense of the word. It's a lack of knowledge. The Corinthian believers have come out of a pagan and idol-worshiping religion. They are used to serving idols that are deaf and mute, but now they serve a living God who desires to speak to them.

In 1 Corinthians 12, Paul patiently shares what the gifts are.

In 1 Corinthians 13, he shows them how to serve with these gifts.

In 1 Corinthians 14, he shows them how to handle spiritual gifts in the right way so as not to create confusion or disorder.

Your Promise: The Holy Spirit Gives Gifts and Makes *You* Stronger

When I was younger, I had a necklace. My friend Kathy owned one just like it—almost. My necklace was half of a heart that said *Best*. Her necklace was the other half, and it said *Friend*. When you put them together, the two halves made a whole.

The spiritual gifts are unique, but they fit together.

They are for the common good of the church. We don't all have the same gifts, no more than a body has only elbows or feet. Each gift has a distinct purpose. No gift is more important than the others.

> To one there is given through the Spirit a message of wisdom, to another a message of knowledge by means of the same Spirit, to another faith by the same Spirit, to another gifts of healing by that one Spirit, to another miraculous powers, to another prophecy, to another distinguishing between spirits, to another speaking in different kinds of tongues, and to still another the interpretation of tongues. All these are the work of one and the same Spirit, and he distributes them to each one, just as he determines.
>
> 1 Corinthians 12:8–11

If we watch the early church closely, we'll start to see how these gifts functioned. Paul certainly operated in the gifts of faith and miracles. John grew from a boisterous, attention-seeking young believer to a man who prophesied about the end of times. When Philip climbed into the chariot with the Ethiopian centurion, he offered a word of knowledge. He was also discerning.

They weren't special because they operated in the gifts. They weren't elevated above anyone else; in fact, they humbly lived their faith in ways that most people wouldn't choose on their own. They believed in the gift Jesus said they would receive. They embraced his role in their faith. They walked and breathed and lived in the gifts of the Holy Spirit.

Spiritual fruit grew in their lives as a result.

But the fruit of the Spirit is love, joy, peace, forbearance, kindness, goodness, faithfulness, gentleness and self-control. Against such things there is no law.

Galatians 5:22–23

While we often discuss the goodness of the gifts, it's the fruit that matters to God.

Your Invitation: Unwrap the Gifts

I love presents. It doesn't have to be anything big. A caramel apple makes me just as happy as tickets for two to the movies. A handwritten note left on my steering wheel or bathroom mirror is an incredible gift.

What if we approached spiritual gifts in the same way?

They've been carefully selected for the church. In many cases, they are the answers to the prayers we've been praying.

God, help me know what to do with this ministry.

Lord, do I play a part?

Father, I want to make a difference.

These gifts are for us. One or more might be for you. One might be for me. They are *all* for the church.

When I first began to study these gifts, I think I expected them to drop into my life like a UPS package on my doorstep. I may have imagined there'd be a sign that would shout, "Today is the day Suzie received discernment." Looking back, I realize that I received spiritual gifts drop by drop over the years.

As I practiced the presence of the Holy Spirit as part of my faith-view, the more individual giftings developed in me. I didn't have a name for what was happening, but my faith increased in a difficult time. It made no sense that I felt so secure in who God was when my world was crumbling around me, but there it was—the gift of faith.

I couldn't explain why I respected that feeling to slow down or to change course when on the outside a situation seemed perfectly fine, but there it was—the gift of discernment.

We can ask God for specific gifts. As I write this, my daughter and mom have cancer. I'm praying for faith. I trust God, but I desire faith that goes before me when I walk through those hospital doors. I'm not telling God what to do with that faith. I'm sitting in his presence, telling him that I long for it.

God knows who we are and the role we play in the church.

He knows the seasons where one gift is critical or will draw people closer to him. Then there are gifts that are consistent for a lifetime. Billy Graham wrote,

> Ask God to show you what specific spiritual gift He has given you. It may be the gift of hospitality; it may be the gift of compassion or help for those in need; it may be some other gift you don't even realize you have. The Bible says, "When he ascended on high, he . . . gave gifts to his people" (Ephesians 4:8).[1]

Like any gift, we can ask for what we want, but this Giver knows us. He has plans we don't even know about—not yet. He sees things, in us and in the body of Christ, that we don't see. It's important to understand that a gift doesn't define the recipient. If we have a specific gift, it doesn't mean we aren't asked to do other things outside that gifting. If I am in a season of leading, and I know it's where I'm supposed to be, I won't shout to the rooftops that serving is not my gifting. Instead, I trust in those seasons that the Holy Spirit will equip me.

It may be that we start to walk in a new gifting.

Rather than worry about what gift we may or may not have, let's

- know the gifts
- embrace the gifts
- hold them loosely, because the gift is always about the Giver

Let's pretend it's a spiritual Christmas and unwrap the gifts Paul describes in 1 Corinthians 12:8–11. This isn't a thorough teaching, but a peek. There are many powerful books that take this deeper, and I hope you'll seek some of them out. But we learn the most as we practice the presence of the Holy Spirit in our everyday lives. We don't have to figure it out on our own, not any more than the early church did.

Our role is to be open to what he desires to give and what he wants us to do. Let's pull the bow off the first gift and take a look.

The gift is valuable because of the Giver.

Wisdom

The spiritual gift of wisdom isn't a head full of knowledge. You can be educated or the smartest person in the room and lack wisdom. This gift is divine wisdom that speaks into the life of a person or a situation, with the goal of drawing that person closer to Christ and his truth.

My husband operates in this gift.

He doesn't tell the world he has the gift of wisdom. He will never stand on a stage and tell the world what to do, but people are drawn to him because of this gift.

He's a counselor today, but he wasn't for the majority of his working life.

He grew up on a farm, then worked at a factory to provide for our family. He went back to school in his late forties to gain his master's degree in counseling and earn a couple of different counseling licenses. Even in the factory, people were drawn to his gentle faith and wisdom. When he served in the church, people often remarked, "Richard knew exactly what to say."

Spiritual wisdom is subtle and marked by humility (James 3:17). The purpose is to bring God's wisdom into a particular situation that affects the body of Christ, or to draw a person closer to God's heart in their situation.

Knowledge

I shared in an earlier chapter that four different people have spoken a word over my life. Those words of knowledge fit within this spiritual gift. They shared something they believed that God gave them—a message for me. This is knowledge that you might not otherwise have for a person or situation. It may also be an invitation for you to intercede (commit to pray) for that person or situation.

A few months ago, I spoke at a women's conference, and mid-message I felt that I was to share a story. I glanced at the clock. I looked at the few notes in front of me. When you speak, your priority is always to honor God, but you also want to honor the time constraints and the people who invited you there. That nudge wouldn't go away. Even as I spoke, I started to pray.

Is this you, Holy Spirit?

It was. I put my few notes aside and obeyed. Later, the women's ministries director pulled me aside.

"How did you know?" she asked.

I had shared my personal testimony about forgiving. It wasn't in my notes, and it wasn't a part of my message for the entire weekend. This is an excerpt of what I shared:

> I was told for years that I *needed* to forgive, but I was truly set free when I discovered that I *get* to forgive. Unforgiveness holds us hostage. It builds walls. If you have held on to a grudge for years, today is the day to put that down. God wants you to be free.

To be honest, I felt a little uncertain sharing this with that particular audience because it was so completely out of the context of the conference theme. Yet the women's ministries leader shared that unforgiveness had hurt many within their ministry. They had taught on it. They prayed about it. The issue remained. I had no idea what was going on in the hearts of the women who prayed arm-in-arm after that message. The women's ministries leader told me, in tears, that many of those who prayed were women who had struggled the most.

I didn't know, but God did.

Perhaps the Lord had me say those words because I was safe. I was a stranger, someone they didn't have to face next week. I came in. I spoke. I left. Somebody else had already done all the hard work, but God allowed me to plant one more seed.

God knew the name of every person in that room. He knew how they had been loved by those in the church. Those same people would be there to love them as they forgave and received what God was trying to give.

A message of knowledge works closely with the gift of wisdom. It's not self-serving. If you feel tempted to go from person to person to tell them all that God finds wrong with them, there's probably a different spirit at work. The spiritual gift is bathed in God's love (1 Corinthians 13:2), and it is at his direction. There is no other agenda but to follow the leading of the Holy Spirit.

Spirit of faith

This gift is an unusual measure of trust in God. It is confidence in who he is. It is a belief that when you pray, he hears and will act on those prayers. You aren't telling God what to do, because you have incredible faith that he is sovereign and already at work.

This gift often accompanies the next two.

Spirit of healing

Can you imagine what it was like to be in the crowd and see Peter pray for a lame man who then stood for the first time in his life? This is why this gift was often coveted in the early church. This gift is a belief that God restores health, whether physical or emotional, through prayer.

It's linked with faith, trusting that God hears our prayers and is at work.

But, Suzie, not all people are healed.

You are right. Lazarus, who was called from the tomb by Jesus, experienced healing. He was raised from the dead—a miracle! Yet he eventually succumbed to either disease or old age.

Jesus prayed for many people, and many were healed, but not everyone was healed.

God receives the glory through healing.

There's also purpose in suffering (Romans 5:3–4; 2 Corinthians 1:3–4).

The spiritual gift of healing isn't believing that, if you say the right words or believe enough, God will react like a genie in a bottle. It's knowing that God does heal. This is a gift I've held on to with my own family in this season. It's never failing to pray as he leads. It's anticipating that he will respond, and trusting the outcome. It's certainty that prayer is powerful and effective—it's faith in the One listening to those prayers.

Miracles

The gift of miracles and wonders results in supernatural acts that can only be explained by God. The apostles prayed for people who were demonically oppressed, and they were set free. Paul and Silas sat in jail singing at the top of their lungs, and their chains fell off as barred doors opened.

This gift is less prominent today, at least in our part of the world. The temptation when a gift is less prominent is to find fault or explain it away. We could do that, or sincerely seek God and ask him to work miracles in us and through the church as he chooses.

When I traveled throughout India, I heard stories of many miracles. It challenged me in my own faith to ask for this gift.

The purpose of miracles has always been to demonstrate the glory of God. Most who had this gift did not seek to produce miracles, but the miracles came as they loved people and ministered exactly as God called them.

Prophecy

This gift is the ability to speak a public message (usually in the church, but it can also be one-to-one) that encourages, comforts, or instructs the body of Christ, or draws unbelievers to the Lord. It is the heart of God spoken in human words, which is why it's so important that any prophetic message be measured against Scripture (1 Thessalonians 5:20–21).

What is the difference between a word of knowledge and prophecy?

A word of knowledge is information about something. Prophecy tells us what to do.

Discernment

This gift is the ability to distinguish between truth and error, between God and the work of the enemy. This is the gift I've been given, and I don't know if I've ever publicly shared that before now. This spiritual gift has shown up over the past three decades in many different ways. I told a story earlier about a man who approached me and Richard to talk about a pastor's message, and how he disagreed with it. He wasn't unpleasant. He expressed that he had genuine concerns. He said he just wanted to hear what I had to say.

My spirit was screaming inside—danger, danger, danger!

That might sound over the top to you, but I respect it when it happens on those rare occasions. God sees something that I don't. He doesn't want me to be a part of it. He wants me to back away, leave it alone, and take it to him to know how to respond and what to do.

In another incident, I was driving down the highway at night. A car pulled up next to me and swerved as though it was going to hit my car. I sped up. There were two men in the car. They pulled behind me and tailed me for nearly a mile. At one point they moved in front of me and slammed their brakes. It was terrifying. We were the only ones on the highway. This was before cell phones (yes, I know, I'm ancient). They finally sped up and zoomed down the road. I took a deep breath. My exit was just ahead, and I started to pull off.

There it was.

Don't.

The problem was that the next exit was nearly five miles away. It was late. I was exhausted and wanted to be home.

Don't.

That feeling inside that I have come to recognize as discernment grew louder.

I kept going.

As I drove over the hill and looked over my shoulder, I saw what I couldn't see earlier. It shook me to my core. The car with the two men was at the end of that exit, waiting in the dark. They couldn't have known this was my exit, but it was a common one. If I had exited as normal, I would have been blocked, unable to get off the road or back onto the highway.

How did my spiritual discernment build the body of Christ that night?

Maybe the fact that I'm writing these words to you right now had something to do with that. I don't know, but I have learned to respect and act on this gift.

Speaking in tongues

This gift is the ability to pray or worship in a language or words that a person doesn't speak in the natural. It's also one of the gifts that the children of God argue most over. Some think that if you don't speak in tongues, you don't have the Holy Spirit. Others believe it was only for the early church. Some want this gift but are afraid of what people will say if they privately or publicly speak in tongues.

Let's address the first one, that if you don't speak in tongues, you don't have the Holy Spirit.

When we don't know what to believe, our first stop is always Scripture. In Acts 1, Jesus promises the early church that they will be filled with his power and be his witnesses (verses 5, 8). Tongues accompany this filling in three different instances in the Bible. In Acts 2, a whoosh like a great wind enters the room. Tongues of fire light on each of them. They speak in languages foreign to their own tongue, and the bystanders below understand what they are saying. In Acts 10 and 19, believers are filled with the Holy Spirit and speak in tongues—and some prophesy.

There are other stories of being filled with the Holy Spirit and his power that don't mention tongues.

For example, in Acts 9:17, a sinful man named Saul is prayed for and filled with the Holy Spirit. There are no tongues of fire or wind, at least none recorded in that initial introduction. Yet a good work began in Saul as scales fell from his eyes, and he walked away a different man.

And in Acts 13:52, Paul and Barnabas are leaving after a disappointing ministry trip. They are *filled* with the Holy Spirit. Rather than tongues, the result is joyful worship as they exit the city.

We know that Paul did speak in tongues, but he described it as one of the many good gifts of the Spirit (1 Corinthians 14).

The second source of conflict about this particular gift is that some believe it was reserved only for the early church. That brings me back to the moment when I knelt at the altar at the age of seventeen, desperate for help, and the Holy Spirit showed up.

When I share that story, people ask what happened. I don't know exactly. For two hours, I worshiped and communed with God in a fresh new way. I walked away knowing that I could live my faith. That experience was the first of many over decades of faith.

For many, tongues is a beautiful form of private and empowering communication (1 Corinthians 14:4).

The gift of tongues can also be expressed in a body of believers. As with all the gifts, it is to encourage the body of Christ. Paul instructs that a public message of tongues is to be accompanied by interpretation of tongues (1 Corinthians 14:27–28).

While speaking in tongues is an incredible gift, Paul said that not everyone will speak in tongues (1 Corinthians 12:30)—though we are all to be filled with the Holy Spirit.

Billy Graham, in his book *The Holy Spirit*, says,

[The Holy Spirit] chooses who gets which gifts, and He dispenses them at His good pleasure. While we are held accountable for the use of any gifts He gives us, we have no responsibility for gifts we have not been given.[2]

Rather than seeing tongues as necessary to being filled with the Holy Spirit, we view the Holy Spirit as necessary to having this or any of his good gifts.

The last concern you might have about this spiritual gift is being afraid of what people will say. That same concern can be shared about any part of your relationship with God, can it not? The risk is that some might not understand what you believe or why you do what you do. The reward, despite that risk, is that you live open to whatever God has for you.

If God has something for you, hold up your hands for every drop and thank him for it.

Interpretation of tongues

This gift allows a person to translate a message in tongues that is spoken publicly. The Greek word for interpretation is *hermeneia,* which means to translate or expand a message not understood in a natural way. A person with this spiritual gift is able to interpret what is being said and communicate it to others. It blesses the church and encourages the listeners. It eliminates confusion.

Spiritual Gifts without Borders

Paul explained the gifts to the early church and went on to teach that we are all in the body of Christ. You. Me. That woman kneeling on a dirt floor singing her heart out in a different language. Big churches. Little churches. Secret churches that meet at great cost.

We need each other. We do!

Now you are the body of Christ, and each one of you is a part of it. And God has placed in the church first of all apostles, second

prophets, third teachers, then miracles, then gifts of healing, of helping, of guidance, and of different kinds of tongues. Are all apostles?
Are all prophets? Are all teachers? Do all work miracles? Do all
have gifts of healing? Do all speak in tongues? Do all interpret?

1 Corinthians 12:27–30

This is how the gifts are used in the church. Some serve. Some lift
people up in encouragement. Some teach. Some preach and shepherd
people as they mature in their faith. Some are truth tellers when it's
not popular to tell the truth. Some drop everything to pray, while
others walk confidently into a world that is messed up, broken,
and in need of a Savior and confidently believe that God is bigger.

The gifts play out in every part of this.

We live a life of love and faith without borders . . . *together.*

The Word

Even so the body is not made up of one part but of many.
Now if the foot should say, "Because I am not a hand, I do
not belong to the body," it would not for that reason stop
being part of the body.

1 CORINTHIANS 12:14-15

Your Spirit-Led Promise

You play a part in the body of Christ.

Your Spirit-Led Invitation

Unwrap the gifts.

Prayer

I'm stopping at the door. I'm not pushing through to rummage through the gifts. I just want to say thank-you for equipping me, for equipping us. There are too many who still don't know who you are, and too many opportunities to live and love without borders.

Help me. Help us.

I'm so grateful.

EPILOGUE

What Now?

The word *epilogue* sounds so fancy.

I wish you were sitting across from me. You might have coffee, one of those drinks with a five-word name like a mocha espresso with a half shot of something or other. I'd have a green smoothie. My worn-out Bible would be close, and yours would be near as well.

Our friendship would begin with our love for our faith.

We have both felt God's love. We have both been rescued by our Savior. We both have a Helper who ignites our faith.

We'd talk about the Helper and what an incredible gift he is.

It's at this point that you'd lean over and ask, "What now?"

It's a fair question.

The Holy Spirit has been a part of my faithview for a very long time, ever since that pivotal moment when I knelt and asked God for help. Writing this book has reminded me of how complicated we sometimes try to make this simple, beautiful gift.

If this is new to you, step into the role of a disciple, for that is what you are.

Jesus said to wait expectantly. I still do that today. If God has good gifts for me that will help me live, breathe, and operate in my faith, I offer my heart willingly. I don't try to define what he wants to give me, but I tell him I want every drop. I don't make it fit my specifications. If he's the one offering it, I want him to cover my head, my heart, my words, my life with that gift.

So first, *linger*.

Slow down long enough in this crazy whirlwind we call life and tell God that you are open to all he has for you. Let him know you want the gift of the Holy Spirit to be integrated with your faith. Be aware that this gift isn't one that makes faith easy; it is an equipping of your faith. The Helper guides, comforts, speaks, and challenges for a purpose.

Second, practice the presence of the Holy Spirit.

One of my favorite writers is a seventeenth-century monk named Brother Lawrence. As a young man, he had a private encounter with God in a garden that led him to begin to "practice the presence" of God. It was his desire to turn even the smallest parts of his day into worship and relationship with his heavenly Father.

He later went on to write a short book. It was his conversation with God, composed of sixteen letters and a list of simple truths he had learned by practicing the presence of God. This book, written by a man who lived in anonymity, has been distributed to millions.

Brother Lawrence believed there was a vast difference between a powerless life and living in the Spirit. He practiced the presence of God as he thought of him by day, by night, in business, and even in the diversions, believing that God is always near and with us.

Practicing the presence of the Holy Spirit is no different. We simply include the truth that we have a Helper as part of our faithview.

When I'm frustrated by what I cannot do on my own, I practice the presence of the Holy Spirit as I seek discernment, wisdom, counsel, boldness, confidence, faith, belief, and all that he is. But let's not wait until we hit the end of ourselves. Like Brother Lawrence, let's invite the Holy Spirit into our day when our feet hit the floor. Let's look for his handiwork and appreciate it.

Last, if we were sitting around the table together or hiking side by side, I'd remind you—because you already know it—that we are the church. We are loved. We are rescued. We have all that we need to follow Jesus wherever he leads.

There's work to do.

God loves us.

Jesus rescued us.

The Holy Spirit helps us live our faith.

There are people who don't know that God's love sets us free. So let's be who we are. Let's love because we are incredibly loved. Let's live our faith and life with confidence, empowered, soaked in truth, bold, directed . . . and as women who were worth fighting for and now fight for others in his name. Let's live a life of love and faith without borders as we embrace the promise of our Helper.

Suzie

THE SPIRIT-LED HEART
STUDY GUIDE

Chapter One: Released from Uncertainty

1. The Holy Spirit is described as the activator of our salvation. He helps us to live out our faith. In what area do you need help?

2. Waiting is never our first instinct, but what might it look like for you to wait expectantly for the Holy Spirit?

3. Read Luke 22:54–62. Describe Peter's confidence crisis. Share one way that you might relate to his fears.

4. In Acts 2:14–41, Peter steps up to speak to the crowd, and there's a response. Name three adjectives that come to mind that describe Peter in this scene. How did the Holy Spirit change Peter?

5. According to Ephesians 4:30, Acts 7:51, and 1 Thessalonians 5:19, we can grieve, quench, and resist the Holy Spirit. Fill in the following blanks with words that counter those: *We can*

bring joy to, _____, *and* _____
the Holy Spirit. Make that your prayer.

6. If the root of a confidence crisis is fear, name that fear. Ask the Holy Spirit to meet you in it. Make it a prayer. Open your heart to whatever he desires to show you.

Visit www.tsuzanneeller.com/SpiritLedHeart to download a printable version of the artwork on the next page.

God loves you.

Jesus rescued you.

The Holy Spirit helps you.

Chapter Two: Power Greater Than Our Own

1. Peter and John could have tossed a few coins to the lame man and gone on their way. In what way was prayer a more personal gift?

2. In 1 John 5:5–6, John the apostle is speaking. He's elderly and has experienced years of persecution and the loss of a brother, as well as many of his friends, for the cause of Christ. Name one way the Holy Spirit helped him during each chapter of his story.

3. Share briefly your *dynamis* story. It might be your life story, or something that took place today.

4. Do miracles still take place today? Share why you answered the way you did.

5. In Acts 4:32–37, believers work together in unity after they are "shaken" by the power of the Holy Spirit. In what way do you long for *dynamis* power to shake you?

6. *Dynamis* power is evident in our lives because Jesus willingly laid down his life. Read Colossians 2:13 and Matthew 27:51. What is your response to these verses?

7. What is one "should" that you'd like to shake from your heart? Ask the Holy Spirit to empower you to rewrite that chapter.

Chapter Three: We Will Live in Truth

1. What is the greatest struggle with knowing what is true and what is not?

2. What is a lie you have believed? Write it down. It could be a lie from the past or a current lie.

3. How does this lie contrast with the Word of God (truth)?

4. Write down a Scripture verse that puts that lie to shame. Speak it out loud. Put your name in the verse.

5. Why might we justify half-truths or gray areas?

6. In 2 Corinthians 6:3–10, Paul the apostle describes the ways they represent their faith in a culture that doesn't welcome it (or them). How does truth play a part in that? Is it important today? Why or why not?

7. "The Holy Spirit leads us to truth. Truth leads to freedom." What does that mean to you personally?

8. Second Timothy 1:14 instructs us to guard the truth. What role might the Holy Spirit play in guarding the truth when it's sometimes seen as an option?

Chapter Four: We Will Never Wander

1. In Acts 13:2–4, the Holy Spirit instructs two followers of Jesus to go in a specific direction. How do they receive these instructions? What does this teach us?

2. Not everybody is supposed to go to a foreign country. Does that make you any less a missionary? Why or why not?

3. In Acts 8:29, Philip receives instructions to walk beside a cart. What happens?

4. Describe how the Holy Spirit might lead us in the same way.

5. We might be tempted to jump ahead of the Holy Spirit's leading. Why is it important to follow his guidance?

6. "Before we ask for the Holy Spirit to direct us, we need to be willing to accept his direction." Share your response to that statement.

Visit www.tsuzanneeller.com/SpiritLedHeart to download a printable version of the artwork on the next page.

God's Truth Replaces Lies with Freedom!

Lie	Truth	Word
This is too big.	I am not asked to do anything without God, and he is always bigger!	Isaiah 55:8–9
I am not worthy.	I am chosen and dearly loved.	Colossians 3:12
No one sees me.	God not only sees me, he knows me.	Luke 12:6–7
I'm weak.	My strength is in the Lord.	Deuteronomy 31:6
I'll never get past the past.	I am holy, redeemed, and restored because I'm God's child.	Ephesians 1:4–7
God can't possibly forgive me.	My sins are removed.	Psalm 103:12
I am not/will never be enough.	God can use even the hard parts of my story for his purpose.	1 Peter 2:9
I'm a terrible person.	I am lovely, and there is no flaw in me.	Song of Songs 4:7
I am a quitter.	God gives me staying power!	Philippians 4:13
My heart will never heal.	Jesus came to heal my broken heart.	Luke 4:18–19
God can't use my life.	He equips me.	Hebrews 13:20–22
I'm in this alone.	I am safe. He covers me and defends me.	Psalm 91:4

Chapter Five: Hope beyond a Quivering Soul

1. Were you surprised by Jesus's words in John 5:30? Why do we try to live our faith alone?

2. Share one area where you need the fellowship of the Holy Spirit.

3. What is the difference between boldness led by the Holy Spirit and boldness that is a part of a person's personality or agenda?

4. Read Acts 22:20. Stephen's boldness is witnessed by Saul, and years later Paul recalls it as part of his testimony. How might Stephen's boldness have played a part in Saul's/Paul's faith story?

5. "Surrender leads to listening, which leads to fellowship, which leads to boldness." Do you agree with that statement?

6. Share a time when you were bold in your faith even though you were afraid.

Chapter Six: We Are Worth Fighting For

1. "You are worth fighting for." Share three words that describe how you feel as you read that statement.

2. Which of the enemy's lies is your greatest battleground?
   - God doesn't care.
   - Why bother with faith?
   - If only God would do something.

3. In Galatians 5:17, Paul describes the conflict between our flesh and the Spirit. How does the Holy Spirit help us in that battle?

4. Imagine the Holy Spirit in a fighting stance in a boxing ring. Who or what is his greatest opponent?

5. What is one way to allow him to fight for you?

6. What is one biblical way to advocate for others?

7. Read Ephesians 6:10–20. How does the Holy Spirit equip you for battle?

Chapter Seven: We Will Know What to Do

1. "We don't know what we don't know." Describe your response to that statement.

2. Paul is called to minister to the Gentiles. What is Peter's role in this new phase for the early church?

3. Describe a time when someone confirmed what the Holy Spirit was already speaking. How did it help you clarify what God was trying to tell you?

4. Read 1 Corinthians 2:1–12. In verses 9–12, Paul describes how the Spirit reveals God's plan. How is the Holy Spirit instrumental in revealing God's plan for you?

5. Look up the definition of an earthly counselor. What are the similarities and differences between that and the Holy Spirit as Counselor?

6. Suzie described the Word as spiritual food, rest, and restoration. In what ways do you need those things today?

Chapter Eight: We Recognize What Is Unseen

1. Why is it valuable to see beyond the obvious? Name some areas of your life where this might be important.

2. Read Acts 15:5–12. What is the response to Paul and Barnabas as they work through the disagreement? What makes this possible?

3. Why do you believe the Holy Spirit is so protective of the church? Do you believe he is protective of you as well? Why or why not?

4. If you feel that the Holy Spirit is grieved by your actions or those of another, what is your natural response? What do you *want* that response to look like? Write that as a personal prayer.

   ....

   ....

   ....

   ....

5. We can give far too much weight to the enemy, or far too little weight to the fact that oppression exists. What is the balance according to Scripture?

Chapter Nine: We Love Our Faith, but We *Live* Our Faith

1. If belief is "surrender," what are we surrendering to as we live our faith?

2. Read 1 Corinthians 2:8–10. What role does the Holy Spirit play in establishing our beliefs?

3. Galatians 4:6 says that we are children of God. If we believe that, how might it change the way we live?

4. What are things that "look like faith" but aren't necessarily faith? Why is it important to know the difference?

5. Read John 16:7–11. We often stress how the Holy Spirit convicts the world of sin, but name one way this also helps those who desire to live their faith.

6. If you were asked why you believe, what would you say? (Take the pressure off. Don't try to be eloquent.)

Chapter Ten: Good Gifts Make Us Stronger

1. Describe the best gift you've ever received. What made it special?

2. There are many people who are wise. What is the difference between natural wisdom and the spiritual gift of wisdom?

3. We sometimes shy away from the Holy Spirit because we have seen abuse of his gifts. Why might this be a mistake?

4. The gift of faith doesn't make any one person a healer. It is a gift of belief that God can heal. Why is that distinction important?

5. If the church operated in these gifts, what might be the result?

6. If the focus of gifts is the Giver, how does that change the way you see those gifts?

ACKNOWLEDGMENTS

I don't believe it's ever easy to write a book, but there are people who make it easier. I'm grateful to my family. Richard, thank you for showing up at that little cottage tucked down a dirt road. You surprised me with delicious chicken from a gas station (it was the only restaurant within miles). I was in the home stretch and needed to hide away for a few days to write. Your presence and sweet words of encouragement made a difference.

I have always loved you, but I delight that I also like you—so much.

I am grateful for Stephen and Leslie, Ryan and Kristin, and Josh and Melissa, plus my wild bunch of six littles. I'm not an author to you. I'm Mom. I'm Gaga. You keep me grounded, and I love that.

My daughter and mom were both diagnosed with cancer while I wrote this book. I can't list all the women who gathered around me and my loved ones in that hard, hard place. You sent cards. You sent sweet little gifts for Leslie's young daughters. You penned healing words to my mom. Every time you touched my loved ones, you were the hands and feet of Christ to this girl. Thank you, Living Free Together friends, for your prayers reached me every day. I am blessed to have you as friends.

Thank you to my friends Holley Gerth and Jennifer Watson, who asked if they could write guest blog posts to fill the gap while I absorbed difficult news. I love our friendship. I love that you knew exactly what I needed.

I am grateful for my Wednesday night Bible study group. We've gathered around the table in my kitchen for four years to talk about Jesus. I am thankful for Cynthia, Angye, Carmen, Onita, Becky, Sharon, Nancy, and Sheila. We eat, laugh, and hold each other up. I'm deeply thankful for each of you.

Thank you to the women of Proverbs 31 Ministries. I rode on the waves of your prayers and treasure our friendship. You make me a better version of myself.

Thank you to The FEDD Agency and team. Esther, there is no one like you, and I'm grateful for you and all the amazing women who work alongside you.

Kim Bangs, you represent the kingdom well. I'm so thankful that you are my editor, and for Bethany House Publishers. This team feels like a family. I know that's rare, and I'm lucky.

Thank you to Susan Addington and her husband for letting me stay rent-free in a little Ozark cottage while finishing this book. I drank cups of hot chocolate, wore yoga pants for days on end, and soaked in a view that declared that God is a magnificent artist. It was a healing place to write days before my daughter's surgery. It calmed this mama's heart and let me reconnect with God in such a powerful way. It allowed the Holy Spirit to speak with each keystroke.

Last, I am grateful for forty years of faith.

God loved me.

Jesus rescued me.

The Holy Spirit helps me live my faith.

What an amazing gift.

Suzie

NOTES

Chapter 1: Released from Uncertainty

1. Martyn Lloyd-Jones, *God the Holy Spirit* (Wheaton, IL: Crossway Books, 1997), 20.

Chapter 2: Power Greater Than Our Own

1. Catherine Marshall, *The Helper: He Will Meet Your Every Need*, Guideposts edition (Lincoln, VA: Chosen Books, 1978), 178.

Chapter 3: We Will Live in Truth

1. Jennifer Rothschild, *Me, Myself, and Lies: What to Say When You Talk to Yourself* (Eugene, OR: Harvest House, 2017), 11.

Chapter 6: We Are Worth Fighting For

1. Tim Keller, *Encounters with Jesus: Unexpected Answers to Life's Biggest Questions* (New York: Riverhead, 2015), 141.
2. Eric Holt Gimenez, "We Already Grow Enough Food for 10 Billion People—and Still Can't End Hunger," *Huffington Post*, May 2, 2012, http://www.huffingtonpost.com/eric-holt-gimenez/world-hunger_b_1463429.html.

Chapter 7: We Will Know What to Do

1. Gregg Levoy, *Callings: Finding and Following an Authentic Life* (New York: Three Rivers Press, 1998), 9.
2. Levoy, *Callings*, 9.
3. C. S. Lewis, *The Screwtape Letters* (New York: Harper One, 2001), 16.

Chapter 9: We Love Our Faith, but We *Live* Our Faith

1. Josh McDowell and Bob Hostetler, *Beyond Belief to Convictions* (Carol Stream, IL: Tyndale House, 2002), 31.

2. A. W. Tozer, *Tozer on the Holy Spirit: A 365-Day Devotional*, comp. Marilynne Foster (Chicago: Moody Publishers, 2015), December 11 entry.

Chapter 10: Good Gifts Make Us Stronger

1. "Answers," Billy Graham Evangelistic Association, January 9, 2014, https://billygraham.org/answer/god-has-given-everyone-gifts-with-which-to-serve-him/.

2. Billy Graham, *The Holy Spirit: Activating God's Power in Your Life* (Nashville: Thomas Nelson, 2000), 168.

Suzanne (Suzie) Eller loves nothing more than watching God work in the hearts of women. She believes that *living free together* allows women to stand shoulder to shoulder across the world, living our faith intentionally and in community.

Suzie is an international speaker with The FEDD Agency. She's the author of ten books, including her devotional, *Come with Me: A Yearlong Adventure in Following Jesus.* She's a featured guest on national television and radio programs and has written hundreds of magazine articles and featured columns.

She has served with Proverbs 31 Ministries for over a decade, writing devotions for P31's *Encouragement for Today,* which reaches over one million women daily. She serves on the International Initiative team. Suzie also mentors writers and communicators through P31's COMPEL Training program.

She has been named one of the Top 100 Christian bloggers, and her blog is a community for thousands of women across the world.

Connect with Suzie

Connect with Suzie at her website, Living Free Together (tsuzanne eller.com), where she blogs and also shares online Bible studies, *21-Day Adventures to Living Free,* free resources, radio encouragement, and free study videos.

To book Suzie for speaking engagements, contact The FEDD Agency, thefeddagency.com/fedd-speaking.

You can also follow Suzie through social media:

f facebook.com/SuzanneEllerP31
🐦 @suzanneeller
▶ youtube.com/suzanneeller

Proverbs 31
MINISTRIES

If you were inspired by *The Spirit-Led Heart* and desire to deepen your own personal relationship with Jesus Christ, I encourage you to connect with Proverbs 31 Ministries.

Proverbs 31 Ministries exists to be a trusted friend who will take you by the hand and walk by your side, leading you one step closer to the heart of God through resources like these:

- Free online daily devotions
- First 5 Bible study app
- Daily radio program
- Books and resources
- Online Bible studies
- COMPEL Writers Training: www.compeltraining.com

Proverbs 31 Ministries
877-731-4663
www.proverbs31.org

More from Suzanne Eller!

Visit tsuzanneeller.com for more information and a full list of her books.

In her warm, conversational way, bestselling author Suzanne Eller shows how, when you take a step away from the uncertainty, the to-do list, the worries and excuses, you take a step toward the One who promises to delight and surprise, who will transform who you are, how you live, and how you impact the world. *Because where you are going is not as important as Who you go with.*

Come With Me

What if Jesus walked up to you right now and invited you to follow him—no questions asked? When the original disciples said yes, they had no idea what that meant. But they had Jesus to walk alongside them— and so do you! Join Suzanne on this thought-provoking, yearlong adventure through Luke, and discover the beauty of following where he leads.

Come With Me Devotional

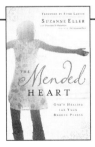

Brokenness happens. When we experience heartache, we often attempt to fix our own brokenness—with disastrous results. If you've tried to heal on your own but keep ending up in the same place, there is good news: Jesus has already completed the work that needs to be done! *The Mended Heart* will encourage you to trust Him, to give and receive grace, and to move ahead even stronger than before.

The Mended Heart

⬙ BETHANYHOUSE

Stay up to date on your favorite books and authors with our free e-newsletters. Sign up today at bethanyhouse.com.

Find us on Facebook. facebook.com/BHPnonfiction

Follow us on Twitter. @bethany_house